THE
Honeysuckle
AND THE
Hazel Tree

"Scène de danse," plate 24 from *Le Remède de la Fortune et Le Dit du Lion*
(Bibliothèque nationale, MS Fr. 1586, fol. 51).
Phot. Bibl. Nat. Paris.

THE

Honeysuckle

AND THE

Hazel Tree

MEDIEVAL STORIES OF

MEN AND WOMEN

———————

TRANSLATED AND

WITH AN INTRODUCTION BY

PATRICIA TERRY

UNIVERSITY OF CALIFORNIA PRESS

BERKELEY   LOS ANGELES   LONDON

University of California Press
Berkeley and Los Angeles, California

University of California Press, Ltd.
London, England

© 1995 by
The Regents of the University of California

Library of Congress Cataloging-in-Publication Data

The honeysuckle and the hazel tree : medieval stories of men and women ;
translated and with an introduction by Patricia Terry.
    p.   cm.
    Includes bibliographical references (p.)
    ISBN 0-520-08378-4 (alk. paper). — ISBN 0-520-08379-2 (pbk. : alk. paper)
    1. Literature, Medieval—History and criticism.   2. Men in literature.
    3. Women in literature.   I. Terry, Patricia Ann, 1929– .
    PN671.H66   1995
    809.1′02—dc20   94-41272
                                                            CIP

Printed in the United States of America

9 8 7 6 5 4 3 2 1

The Nightingale, The Two Lovers, Honeysuckle, Eliduc, The Reflection, and
The Chatelaine of Vergi appeared in slightly different versions in *Lays of Courtly Love,*
trans. Patricia Terry (Garden City, NY: Doubleday Anchor Books, 1963).

The paper used in this publication meets the minimum requirements of American
National Standard for Information Sciences—Permanence of Paper for Printed
Library Materials, ANSI Z39.48-1984. ∞

To Robert and Nicolas

CONTENTS

PREFACE AND ACKNOWLEDGMENTS

SIX OF THE POEMS TRANSLATED here were previously published as *Lays of Courtly Love* (1963), now out of print. Major changes have taken place in medieval studies during the last thirty years: as their interests have become less philological and more literary, medievalists have turned to close textual analyses, while feminist interpretations and the contributions of historians have further increased our understanding. I have revised my translations accordingly, often toward the more literal.

I would like to emphasize, however, that these translations are not intended to serve the purposes of scholars requiring a word-by-word version. Although I have tried to follow the text in all its detail, my principal aspiration has been to reproduce the literary experience of reading the poems. For most people in the Middle Ages, this would have been an aural experience. In a scene in Chrétien's *Yvain,* a young lady sits in an orchard, reading a romance aloud to her parents. It used to be a familiar part of family life for literary works to provide entertainment in just this way. My translations will function best if they are, at least in part, read aloud. Their prevailing rhythm will then be apparent, particularly if the rhymes are neither overstressed nor minimized.

Two poems have been added to this collection in response to a new interest in their subjects: few narratives treat violence against women as impressively as *Philomena,* a work scarcely thought of in 1963. *Lanval*'s is a vision of female power, benevolent but opposed to the prevailing, patriarchal, society. But none of the authors represented here is concerned with presenting a fixed point of view as an argument in favor of one moral stance or another. The stories they tell have the ambiguity of life itself, their apparent values changing with our perspective. The reader need only try to see them whole.

THIS WORK BEGAN as a doctoral dissertation sponsored by Lawton P. G. Peckham, in whose Columbia University course I began to study Old French. I remember gratefully its Anchor Book editors, Carl Morse, who first welcomed the book, and Eugene Eoyang, whose enthusiasm for rhymes led to revisions.

This new edition has benefited from the contributions of many. Nancy Vine Durling's accurate reading and informed concern for the text increased my aspiration to accuracy. She is responsible for the presence of *Philomena*. To Harriet Spiegel, Minnette Gaudet, Renate Blumenfeld-Kosinski, and Nicolas and Robert Terry, I owe thanks for useful suggestions; to Doris Kretschmer at the University of California Press, my gratitude for championing the project and for her patience. Rose Vekony has been the book's meticulous copy editor, to whom I am indebted for many improvements. Patricia Stirnemann led me through the mazes of Paris libraries to find the cover illustration, and nothing could have been more enjoyable. Finally, I don't commit anything to print without the advice of Elena Aguilar Koster and Kathleen Micklow, whose responses never fail to surprise and enlighten me; their friendship is built in to all my work.

INTRODUCTION

Only your kisses
Can restore my heart to life.
Oh Amon, let me keep what I've found
For all eternity.[1]

(anonymous Egyptian lyric, ca. 1330 B.C.)

POETS HAVE ALWAYS EVOKED the gods, gods appropriate to the prevailing human needs. When there is leisure and prosperity enough, poems begin to express personal rather than communal encounters with the forces beyond our control, such as fear and desire. So, in the troubadour poems of southern France, love itself becomes a deity, ennobling the lover and turning his frustrated passions into gratifying songs. The troubadour tradition died out as a result of the Albigensian Crusade, but not before it had convinced the northern French writers that love was a subject at least as compelling as war.

The earliest extant troubadour poems are the work of Guillaume, who in 1086 became the ninth duke of Aquitaine. In one of his songs he complains that Love will never reward him because he desires what he cannot have.[2] And yet he is not without hope: the heart will gain power from patience. To be acceptable to Love, the lover must be humble. He must also behave properly at court and take care that his speech be decorous. In the next stanza, identical in its complex form to the others, Guillaume abruptly turns to praise of his own

I

skills as a literary craftsman and musician. Then, in the envoi, he sends the poem to represent him to the lady he dare not seek out himself.

What the troubadour poems add to the vast literature of love is the connection between the lover and aristocratic society. The practitioner of what the poets refer to as *fin' amor* must have "a gentle heart," must be, in the sense of the word that persists in our own times, a gentleman.[3] Private experience—the sudden, magical, encounter with the beloved—transforms the lover not only inwardly but also in his relationship to others.[4] His courtesy is in that sense natural and sincere.

So too is his praise of the lady. In Guillaume de Lorris's *Roman de la Rose,* the Lover looks into the Pool of Narcissus and sees the Rose. Maurice Valency writes, "In the superlative worth of his lady, the lover finds the surest guarantee of his own preeminence, more particularly if his love is returned. The lover's compliments, like all self-flattery, are therefore utterly sincere. The lady, while he loves her, is for him really the loveliest and best of women, for it is in terms of his own self-love that he sees her, and we know what power to transform is residual in that."[5] When the troubadour Guillaume calls attention to the elegance of his song, he puts the lover's humility in its place.

The lover suffers from his lady's absence, or her rejection, and is terrified in her presence, but the key word in the troubadour's description of love is *joy.* Guillaume IX wrote an entire poem around *joy,* saying that it cannot be found "in will or desire, in thought or in meditation,"[6] and that nothing compares to it. *Joy* refers also to courteous social behavior; the lover, even in anguish, does not impose his mournfulness on others. *Joy* expresses his gratitude to Love, who may yet allow him that other joy, when the lady grants him her *drudari* and his hands reach under her cloak.[7]

Neither the art of Guillaume IX nor the concept of *fin' amor* could have arisen without antecedents. Various suggestions have been made about possible sources, one of which is Arabic poetry. There are clear resemblances between the strophic meters of Latin religious poems and the forms used by Guillaume and later troubadours.[8] Guillaume calls his lady *mi dons,* "my lord," and Gilbert Highet points out that Latin poets, beginning with Catullus, "call their mistresses *dominae,* and practice or advise complete subjection to the will of the beloved."[9]

Whatever gave rise to the troubadour poems had little effect on the literature of northern France. There, during the first half of the twelfth century, poetry was mainly devoted to warriors, whose love was all for the emperor or their comrades or even for God, but certainly not for women. Count Roland, dying on the battlefield and remembering his life, had no thought for Aude, the woman he was to marry and who would die when she heard of his death.

By the mid-twelfth century, northern poets called *trouvères* were creating their own version of the troubadour tradition, and the warriors of the chansons de geste were beginning to fall in love. The *roman,* or romance—a long narrative poem in octosyllabic couplets—became the dominant literary genre. The word *roman* referred to the vernacular language, which was increasingly used in place of Latin in literature. Because the subjects of the earliest romances were drawn from classical antiquity, the *roman* is "Roman" as well. The medieval authors' adaptation of their sources made romance in the sense of "love interest" central to the European narrative tradition. In Homer's *Iliad,* Briseis is simply a prize of war. Benoît de Ste-Maure, in *The Romance of Troy* (ca. 1165), causes the Trojan hero Troilus to fall in love with her. When she is to be returned to her Greek father, Troilus and Briseida swear undying love, but Briseida succumbs to the eloquence of Diomedes, and Troilus dies in despair.[10] In Virgil's *Aeneid,* Lavinia is "a quiet dutiful passive little girl."[11] In *The Romance of Aeneas* (anonymous, ca. 1160), she initiates a passionate love affair.

In lyric poetry the lady's role is passive: she is the source of a man's aspiration. But in a romance the characters have to interact, even if the story is primarily the knight's. There had of course been lyric poems in the woman's voice, including the earliest fragments of medieval vernacular poetry.[12] In Provence there were some twenty known women troubadours, *trobairitz,* their poems similar in theme to those of the men but considerably more personal in expression.[13] In Old French dances and weaving songs, whose authors and even their approximate dates remain unknown, women joyfully proclaim their ability to triumph over loveless and brutal marriages. But the romances introduced elaborate analyses of young people overcome by unfamiliar emotions. These are the tentative first steps toward the French psychological novel.

The enhanced status of women in literature had little equivalence in real life.[14] Recent studies have shown that women in the twelfth century were more disenfranchised than they had been during the Roman Empire and under Germanic law.[15] The marriage laws to which they were subject were more constricting; wives were valued simply as property. It is a basic principle of *fin' amor* that love cannot exist without freedom. But this is, for the most part, the freedom of men. Courtly love, says Georges Duby, is a man's game,[16] although few could have been as aggressive as Guillaume IX, who said to a bald papal prelate, "The comb will curl the hair on your head before I put aside the vicomtesse."[17]

The performance of courtly song was part of the fabric of courtly society. Literature, at least, deferred to women, as well as to their aesthetic preferences, especially when reinforced by their patronage. Southern attitudes traveled north with Eleanor of Aquitaine, granddaughter of Guillaume IX. She married Louis VII of France, and later Henry Plantagenet, king of England. Her opinions and those of her daughter, Marie de Champagne, were evoked (or invented) by Marie's chaplain Andreas, whose *De Arte Honeste Amandi* (Art of Courtly Love) imitates the style, and perhaps the irony, of Ovid's *Ars Amatoria* (Art of Love). But the courtly literature written by men reflects their interests rather than those of women, however influential these may have been.[18]

Marie de Champagne was the patroness of Chrétien de Troyes, who made King Arthur's court the ideal of twelfth-century aristocracy, displacing its earlier models derived from ancient Greece and Rome. Before Chrétien, Geoffroy of Monmouth had described Arthur's court in his fictional *History of the Kings of Britain* and briefly expressed what would be the new connection between women and warriors: "Nor would they deign have the love of none save he had thrice approved him in the wars . . . [and the knights were] the nobler for their love."[19]

In Chrétien's romances, the Celtic magic of Arthurian legend gives a compelling charm to contemporary problems that remain relevant today. Chrétien wrote most often of conjugal love, attempting to reconcile *fin' amor* and the facts of marriage. In *Erec and Enide,* Enide is given to her future husband by her father, who certainly doesn't request her opinion. He essentially says to Erec, an advantageous match, "Here! She's yours." But Chrétien goes on to describe the passionate relationship of the young couple, whose difficulties in adjusting stem precisely from Erec's failure to distinguish between a lover and a wife. A period of estrangement allows their reconciliation to be not only romantic in feeling but also propitious for the continued harmony of their marriage. As John Stevens says, "They are renewed with all the freshness of new love."[20] The trials they have passed through have also brought them awareness of the place of that love in relation to social responsibility. Similarly in *Yvain,* a man's obligations to his work—doing knightly deeds and maintaining his reputation—conflict with obligations to wife and home. Chrétien's *Philomena* (included in the present volume), explores the dark side of love. In this non-Arthurian work, derived from Ovid, the treatment of the female characters is remarkably sympathetic compared to that of Chrétien's source.

ALMOST NOTHING IS really known about Marie de France. The name we give her comes from the epilogue to her *Fables,*[21] where she calls herself Marie and says that she is "de France" (from France). She was probably living in England at the time, and the king to whom she dedicates the *Lais* may have been Henry II, the husband of Eleanor of Aquitaine. She was clearly at ease in courtly society, whether or not she lived "in the world," and was well educated. In the first *lai* in her collection, she addresses herself with confidence to an audience of noble lords: "Oez, seigneurs, ke dit Marie" (Hear, my lords, what Marie has to say).[22]

Marie seems to have begun writing the *lais,* which Stevens aptly calls "short story romances,"[23] somewhat before the first of Chrétien's *romans.* Her influence was certainly less extensive than his, and the scope of her works is narrower, but few writers have been her equal in quality. She does not invent stories but retells them in a style that seems transparent in its simplicity, yet her versions escape restrictive interpretation. She asserts the value of love for women as well as for men. As Joan Ferrante writes, love in the *lais* "is more than a force that inspires the lover and gives him a new sense of himself; it is also a means of overcoming the pains of the world. It frees the lover's imagination from the bonds that society imposes on it, and it is a gift that women can partake of as fully as men."[24]

TOWARD THE END of the twelfth century, Jean Renart introduced a new kind of romance, one with a much greater emphasis on details of everyday life. In his earliest known work, *L'Escoufle* (The Kite), a pair of very young lovers are separated and make their way in the world without the help of money or their aristocratic families. The young woman supports herself by doing embroidery and by giving shampoos to noblemen.²⁵ The hero of *Guillaume de Dole* fights in ordinary tournaments, distinguishing himself, of course, but not without bruises. His sister emerges from a sheltered life to defend herself in court, recovering her threatened honor by a bold and ingenious ruse.

The latter work's inclusion of lyric poems was widely imitated, but otherwise Jean Renart was not taken as a model. His audience may have missed the distancing quality of an Arthurian setting. His irony, often aggressive and hard to evaluate, may also have been negatively perceived. Judging from the number of extant manuscripts, Jean Renart's shorter work, *Le Lai de l'ombre* (here translated as *The Reflection*), was more successful. It is an unidealized representation of courtship in refined society—or, more exactly, seduction.

In all the works mentioned above, the author's voice suggests multiple points of view; even when the narrative ends unhappily, there is a sense that things could have been otherwise. Writing of Tristan and Iseut, Marie selects a nontragic aspect of their story. But in *La Chastelaine de Vergi*, for which Stuip gives 1240 as a probable date,²⁶ alternative endings are totally excluded, notwithstanding authorial comment. Misfortune, as predicted in the prologue, is the inevitable consequence of the failure to keep love secret. *La Chastelaine de Vergi* was enormously successful, surviving in a variety of forms in several languages until the original text was rediscovered in the early nineteenth century. It might be said to participate in the evolution of the idea of "romance" toward the more somber beauty that Rousseau called *romantique*.

IN THE INTRODUCTION to his *Cligès,* Chrétien lists "The Metamorphosis of the Hoopoe, the Swallow, and the Nightingale" among his works. The poem to which he refers is *Philomena.* This text came to light only in 1885, when Gaston Paris found it embedded in a fourteenth-century work called *L'Ovide moralisé,* with an allegorical interpretation attached.

Jean Frappier's *Chrétien de Troyes* devotes to *Philomena* only a very few pages.[27] These, however, emphatically attribute the work to Chrétien, despite the doubts of other critics. The question of authorship was the topic of most interest in studies of the poem until the 1980s, when feminist readers began to examine the importance of the legend itself, from its earliest literary expressions in ancient Greece.

Book 6 of the *Metamorphoses* begins with Arachne and ends with Philomela. Ovid writes of Arachne with considerable sympathy. She was foolish to enter into a weaving competition with Athena, but in fact she won the contest. Dante includes Arachne among his symbols of pride,[28] and indeed it is her presumptuousness that is said to have evoked the goddess's rage. But Athena's violence seems entirely out of proportion. She destroys Arachne's weaving, beats her until she hangs herself—or is lynched[29]—and finally turns her into a spider. Ovid tells us without comment what was depicted on Arachne's loom: women being raped by gods disguised as beasts. Feminist critics have been more inclined to speculate on the connection between Arachne's subject and the goddess's wrath, Athena being, as Patricia Joplin reminds us, "an extension of Zeus." As Joplin puts it, "For Arachne to tell the most famous tales of women raped by the gods is for her to begin to demystify the gods (the sacred) as the beasts (the violent)."[30] But the subject matter of the weaving was presumably Ovid's contribution. Arachne had assumed that the standards of craftsmanship applied equally to gods and to humans; what she depicts would suggest that her standards of morality should also apply to the acts of divinities. Europa and the other victims do not appear to be flattered by the attentions of the rapists—another cause, perhaps, of Athena's wrath.

Weaving in the story of Philomela is much more obviously a means of communication;[31] nevertheless, Ovid gives the weaver only the plainest materials and does not elaborate on the pictorial representation of her rape and mutilation. When Chrétien rewrites Ovid's text, taking full advantage of the freedom given translators in his day, he makes us aware of Philomena's extraordinary skill, both in his initial description of her and later on, when her weaving involves many colors and an intricate design.

The critic Geoffrey Hartman understands Philomena's victory as "a triumph of Art itself." Joplin would reclaim for "the voice of the shuttle" its own specific occasion:[32] the woman reduced to silence when she would most desire to speak, and finding in her art a source of power. We can only speculate about why Chrétien was attracted to this story, but considering the changes he made in Ovid's text and the treatment of women in his subsequent works, it would seem that both these views of Philomena were part of his intention. He may also have been interested in the story as a corrective to the contemporary enthusiasm for Love.

In Ovid's version, Philomela is simply a beautiful girl—like a naiad, but much better dressed. Chrétien describes her beauty in a long formal portrait, omitting Ovid's humorous remark, and gives equal space to an enumeration of all that Philomena *knew*. Her *savoir* includes games and amusements, falconry, embroidery, the literary arts—reading and writing both verse and prose—music, and effective speech.[33] Her conversations with Tereus, which similarly have no equivalent in Ovid, show her as self-possessed and intelligent.

Pandion's speeches in praise of his daughter are certainly to her honor, although he himself may appear self-indulgent and even improper in his attachment to her.[34]

Tereus sees Philomena as an object of desire; for him her *savoir* has not the slightest importance. But he selects as a guard an old woman whose *savoir* will be the tyrant's undoing. Not only is she skilled in embroidery, thus providing both incentive and materials, she is also compassionate, obeying the letter of Tereus's requirements but increasingly sympathetic to his prisoner, about whom she had asked many questions.[35] Tereus, says the author, had foolishly answered them, no doubt assuming the old woman would be indifferent. To include this conversation, Chrétien had to sacrifice plausibility: if Tereus had indeed told her the truth, the old woman should have recognized what was pictured in Philomena's weaving.

Tereus becomes obsessed with Philomena the instant he sees her. Ovid explains that Tereus is a barbarian from Thrace, and therefore passionate by nature. Several of Chrétien's additions to Ovid's text seem similarly intended to make Tereus appear less reprehensible. When Philomena first appears, Chrétien tells us that she did not look like a "veiled nun," which seems to suggest that she would have done better to make herself less attractive, more inclined toward piety. Even more striking is the passage that evokes an imaginary pagan law, not found in Ovid: Tereus's seduction of his sister-in-law would have been within his rights had she been his sister instead (219–33). His transgression, then, is only a kind of technicality.[36] The irresistible power of love, lengthily described in Ovidian terms, sweeps Tereus away into madness; he is, from that point of view, a victim.[37]

But one has the impression that in the very act of articulating this doctrine, Chrétien loses faith. He contradicts himself, complaining that there is in love itself a lack of wisdom (419–48) and then stating that love is *not* insanity (491–92).[38] Tereus shows that he can still listen to Reason by giving up his plan to abduct Philomena. When she is entirely in his power, he tries, briefly, to persuade her to grant him her love freely. But once the rape occurs, and the subsequent mutilation, both Love and Reason vanish from Chrétien's story.

Ovid tells us that Tereus had intervened to save Athens at a time when Pandion had no other allies, having failed to offer help to the neighboring kingdoms in their time of need. Procne was a kind of return gift, and no one, of course, asked whether she was pleased to marry a barbarian. Ovid has her flirting with her husband, but Chrétien shows her as simply deferential, and concerned lest he be distressed by her desire to visit her sister. Chrétien gives us no indication that Procne has a capacity for violence. She says nothing whatsoever when Tereus insists, without explanation, on going to Greece himself. We might, of course, imagine that her silence conceals many thoughts.

But when Tereus returns without Philomena, Procne turns his lying words to Pandion (530–536) into a self-fulfilling prophecy: she will indeed have nothing further to do with him, and he will indeed lose his son. The funeral rites she performs strangely combine Christian and pagan beliefs, but her intensity in observing them does not hint at the murderous rage she later displays. Chrétien rejects Ovid's portrayal of Procne disguised as a bacchante, a scene that connects her subsequent acts with ritual frenzy. Ovid's Procne is concerned only with revenge, debating the choice of means. In Chrétien's version she realizes that she *has* no means and prays that God will provide some (1288–91). It is at this instant that Itis, looking so much like his father, comes into the room. Even the act of murder is less gruesome than in Ovid; Procne is not compared to a tigress with a fawn, and Philomena does not wield a knife herself, although she does share in the preparation of the meat.

The transformation of Tereus and the sisters into birds comes from the Greek tradition. Ovid's Tereus becomes a warlike hoopoe; the other two birds are identified only by their habitat and united in a lurid description: "Such birds have stains of murder on their breasts / In flickering drops of blood among their feathers."[39] Chrétien states without comment that Procne became a swallow, but he gives to Philomena fifteen lines that restore her voice and define her particular way of bearing witness, of seeking revenge. Like the artfully woven tapestry that reveals a hidden wrong but is not in itself an instrument of justice, the nightingale sings that traitors deserve shame and death. She grieves for the betrayal of innocent women but sings as sweetly (*doucemant*) as she can, luring us closer to unbearable truths.

In Greek legend it is Procne who becomes the nightingale, and her song is "Itys, Itys."[40] "Oci, oci," which became the traditional cry of the nightingale in Old French, seems to have originated with Chrétien.[41] *Oci* has been uniformly understood as the imperative "kill," but it also may be a past participle, suggesting Philomena's cry of regret or lamentation.

IN MARIE DE FRANCE'S *The Nightingale,* the bird is itself a fiction within the fiction, but it is trapped in surrounding realities and slain. In the prologue to the *Lais,* Marie says that she often stayed awake at night writing her stories. Readers have noticed a resemblance to the lady of *The Nightingale,* who stayed awake to commune with her lover and who may or may not have been listening to the bird's song. The beginning of the *lai* praises both husband and lover, whose *bunté* (goodness, benevolence) "gave the city its good name" (11). But the husband is not otherwise commended, and his relationship with his wife is noticeably formal. The *bacelers*—a young, un-

married man of the knightly class—is said to be valiant and generous. "He loved his neighbor's wife" (23), and she fell in love with
him because of his reputation and the eloquence of his courtship, and
because he lived next door. Marie's practicality makes one smile—
and at the same time remember that for a wife imprisoned in her
marriage, happiness would have to be "next door," if at all.

Similarly, they are said to love *sagement,* which could be either
"wisely" or "without taking any chances." But this story takes place
in the real world, where nothing magical will come to the rescue.
The lady is closely watched, and her husband, as we are shown, can
be violent. So the young man, when he isn't at tournaments, is content to talk with his love at her window; and she takes such delight
in his presence that she goes to her window too often. There are
no ironic overtones when Marie describes their meetings, which resemble those of Eliduc and Guilliadun:

> . . . Never wild
> Or frivolous, they kept to mild
> Pleasures of courtship, talked and sent
> Gifts to each other, well content
> To be together when they could.
> (*Eliduc,* 577–81)

It is the lady in *The Nightingale* who distinguishes the nightingale
from springtime birds in general, perhaps without thinking of the
Metamorphoses. Guigemar, the first story in Marie de France's collection,
also features a lady whose husband has enclosed her in a strong house,
and a more precise reference to Ovid. On the walls of the lady's bedroom a mural depicts Venus throwing Ovid's books into a fire and
"excommunicating" those who would follow his teachings. Scholars
have given these lines, and also Marie's opinion of ancient authors as

expressed in the prologue, conflicting interpretations, but as Nancy
Vine Durling writes, it does seem "appropriate that in this passage a
powerful female figure replace Ovid."[42] In Marie's nightingale story,
the violence comes entirely from the husband and is, although dis-
tressing, primarily symbolic. It does not lead to further violence. The
silenced nightingale, wrapped in a cloth on which something has
been written or embroidered, tells its story.

Interpretations of *The Nightingale* vary widely. At one extreme is
John Fowles: "We have all known of the not very daring *affaire* between two overromantic egos that ends up as a dead bird in a precious casket, more treasured for its failure than lamented for its lack
of courage." Glyn S. Burgess takes an intermediate view: "Her
ephemeral relationship provides her with a happiness spiced with
risk, but she is finally left with nothing but her memories and her
embroidery." Jacques Ribard understands what is seen from the
lady's window as a glimpse of the unknown—another world, the object of a spiritual quest, never abandoned and never to be accomplished.[43]

Marie teaches that the story transcends the conflicting views it
may engender. One may say that *The Nightingale*'s lovers lack courage, but one could equally well argue that resignation is, in the real
world, their only possible response. To put the dead bird in a reli-
quary is a pathetic sacrilege; yet the gesture in itself is a commitment to the value of shared love, as opposed to the brutal emotions of
the husband. Either way, the glittering casket preserves and evokes
the story, not as it would have been told by the lover himself, but
made treasurable by literary art.

IN *THE TWO LOVERS*, the dominating male figure is a father rather
than a husband, and the feelings of the daughter include a reluctance
to hurt him. The test he devised for her suitors is neither glamorous

nor heroic, and when the princess falls in love she finds a practical means of enabling her lover to succeed. Some readers admire her good sense. Others think she should have been more adventurous: the boy had tried to persuade her to elope. Nevertheless, he accepts her more moderate solution, and when he starts his climb is fully resolved to use the strengthening potion. Marie tells us it will be of no use to him, because "he has no sense of moderation (*mesure*) at all." In fact, the reasonableness he did have is lost in the joy of holding the maiden in his arms and of reaching the halfway point. But that joy kills them both.

Like *The Nightingale,* this *lai* has often seemed to be making a moral statement. Paula Clifford, for example, says that "the tragic outcome, due to his rejecting the magic potion, is made quite clear by Marie . . . , who relates it specifically to the lack of *mesure*."[44] Other critics admire the youthful spirit, the heroic self-confidence, and the desire to succeed without help, or perhaps a sense that otherwise it would be cheating. The *lai* makes grandiose allusions to Roland and to Iseut; some see this as mocking, while for others it gives the children heroic stature. Robert Hanning and Joan Ferrante believe that Marie deliberately overloads the slender tale in order to "urge the fragility of the literary tradition of ennobling, tragic love."[45]

Yet it seems to me that balance is the essence of Marie's art. When she writes of the boy that "To become the best knight anywhere / Was what he wanted most to do" (52–53), the statement carries a positive and negative charge at once. Similarly, there would have to be both timidity and affection in a young girl's choice not to run away from home. Hanning and Ferrante, who admire the *lai* as self-parody, nevertheless conclude: "The refusal of the potion is at once the triumph and the death of childhood's exalted vision—but the acceptance of the potion would spell the end of the illusion from another point of view."[46] Marie's synthesis of lucidity—the spirit of comedy—and tenderness for the humans so clearly observed is dominant in her work and is a rare literary accomplishment.

WITHIN THE STORY of Tristan and Iseut, *Honeysuckle,* Marie's shortest *lai,* shows the lovers in separation and then briefly together, thanks to Tristan's inscription on a branch from a hazel tree or, in other readings, on the tree itself. What Tristan wrote, says the text, was *sun nun*—"his name," unless it is *"her* name."[47] Lovers usually inscribe the name of the beloved. It would be dangerous to reveal the presence of "Tristan"; indiscreet to write "Iseut." Critics have put forth a number of ingenious speculations, but the ambiguity of *sun nun* corresponds to the fused identity of the lovers, as does our uncertainty about which of them the vine represents and which the tree. What the text makes clear is that the message was meant for Iseut alone.

Reference to the twining vine and the tree is included in "la summe" (the contents, or a summary) of a different message, a written one that Tristan had earlier sent to the queen (61–76). Michelle Freeman observes that as Marie gives us this version of Tristan's words, her "voice blends, or interlaces, with Tristan's."[48] The couplet that follows, in Tristan's words (77–78), gives us a hint of what his own *lai* would have been like, presumably composed in Wales after this secret meeting (107–13). Called *Gotelef* or *Chevrefoil,* its words and music gave expression to Tristan's remembered joy and recorded the *paroles*—the words of the lovers—that Marie's *lai* alludes to but does not reveal.

LANVAL AND *ELIDUC* are less elusive on the subject of love; their culminating mystery is instead a form of Grace. Although different in scope and milieu, they have similar plots. Both portray a great lord

who mistreats an exemplary vassal. Isolated then from society—
Eliduc leaves his home and goes into exile, while Lanval is already
abroad and lacking friends—each is offered a gift of love. Each com-
mits an unpardonable transgression and finds a seemingly impossible
forgiveness. There is no explanation of that mercy.

Among Marie's *lais,* only *Lanval* takes place at King Arthur's
court, which traditionally represents the best the human world can
offer. The son of a foreign king, Lanval has entered the service of
King Arthur and distinguished himself in his wars, only to be forgotten when the knights are rewarded. Lanval, who has been generous, finds himself without resources.

Alone in a meadow, disconsolate, he is approached by two maidens who invite him to their mistress's opulent tent. The boundary of
the Other World of Celtic legend is indicated by a nearby stream and
by the trembling of Lanval's horse. The lady's beauty, unearthly in its
perfection, shows her to be a *fée,* as does her prior knowledge of Lanval. She has come from her distant country to seek him, and asks only
that he return her love and promise to keep it secret. There is no
courtship, no period of testing. Lanval needs only a moment in her
presence to love absolutely. She is perfectly responsive to his sexual
desires, and her gifts solve all the practical problems of his life, but
wonders such as these could possibly be found in the human realm.
What truly matters to Lanval is something in the quality of his
experience, through the *fée,* of the Other World, an experience that
Marie's text surrounds with evocative silence.[49]

Arthur's wife, unnamed in the *lai,* is attracted by Lanval's new
prominence at court, and she too offers her love. No doubt the shock
of the difference between the *fée* and the queen, in manner as well
as in beauty, can account for Lanval's hasty reply when the queen, in
her fury at being rejected, insults him. He boasts of his lady, betray-
ing the secret. It seems clear that the *fée* will never reappear. What
follows shows Lanval's total commitment to his love. The trial that

will condemn him has no importance; all that matters is what he has lost.

Eliduc, also a foreigner in service to a king, is similarly offered a love he did not seek, by a princess he loves in return. Unlike Lanval, who seems entirely worthy of the *fée,* Eliduc is weak at best. He cannot bring himself to tell the princess he has a wife; he neither rejects nor really responds to her advances. Having been falsely accused of treachery by his first lord, he now behaves dishonorably to another.[50] A list of his evasions and misdeeds would make it seem impossible that the reader could feel any sympathy for him at all. He refrains only from physical adultery. But Marie leads him so slowly from one, fairly excusable, fault to another that he seems to be trapped without any decent way out, as the princess continues to trust him and his wife waits at home. Finally eloping with the maiden, who has said that otherwise she would die, he has no plan beyond some kind of hope for the best. Because his desperation is so close to madness, the murder of a sailor, who in revealing Eliduc's marriage caused Guilliadun's apparent death, can be made to seem only a detail.

The title of this *lai,* as Marie tells us at the beginning, is really *Guildelüec and Guilliadun,* the similar names of the women. Like those who realized that the beauty of Lanval's *fée* justified his presumed insult to the queen, Guildelüec, looking at the dead girl, understands her husband's inexplicable grief and shares it. Thanks to a strange little miracle with its own components of violence and love, Guildelüec revives the maiden, who then tells her story, reproaching men for their betrayals.

When Arthur's court is about to condemn Lanval, the *fée,* in an act of truly royal generosity, makes herself visible to all. Even more than in her own white and gold, there is magic in the extremely slow pace of her pure white horse, in the presence of sparrowhawk and hound. The king and his vassals are eager to do her honor, but nothing they can offer is relevant. She exonerates Lanval as far as the king's justice is concerned, but of his real betrayal she says nothing, nor does she look at him. The omission points to what is involved when Lanval leaps on the back of the *fée*'s horse. This gesture, which some readers have found awkward, perfectly represents an act of faith, a crossing of the boundary to the Other World, where Lanval's own skills and knowledge cannot take him. With no guarantees, even of forgiveness, Lanval rejects Arthur's court and goes with the *fée* to Avalon, from which no one ever returns. The similarity of that name to his suggests that it is Lanval's true homeland.

As Guilliadun resembles the *fée* in her beauty, Guildelüec is like her in generosity, bestowing her gifts as if that were perfectly natural and required no comment. She restores Guilliadun to life and happiness, allowing her husband to make a marriage of love. Her benevolence shows the way toward a spiritual domain beyond the pleasures of the world. Eliduc and Guilliadun will follow her; they live in "perfect love," devoting themselves increasingly to good works, and finally renounce secular life.[51]

THE PROTAGONIST OF Jean Renart's *The Reflection* is the very definition of a man-of-the-world: handsome, generous, skilled in tournament fighting, sophisticated in manner, successful with women;

> With many he was wont to make
> Division of his heart, true lover
> To none . . .
>
> (134–36)

Now he sees a woman he truly desires, and finds that his charm, his looks, his elegance are working against him. Courtly love requires a courtly facade, a stylized expression of devotion, which might or might not have its source in the real thing.

The lady, who has been living an irreproachable life for a long time, is not averse to the idea of taking a lover but naturally wants to be sure that the candidate is worthy.[52] Knowing the knight's reputation, she is pleased when he calls on her, yet wary. He tells her the truth: that no other woman matters to him anymore, and he hopes that she will save him from the cruel torments of love. She replies:

> My lord, I would be most surprised
> If it could in fact be true
> That any man who looked like you
> Was pining for love . . .
>
> (378–81)

He reacts to the implied compliment by suggesting that the welcoming expression in her eyes is a truer indication of her feelings than her words, at which she rejects him utterly as a boor.

To recover from his blunder the knight uses a great many words of his own, but nothing he can say or promise has any effect. What does impress the lady, however, is the sight of his blush and the tears mingling red and white on his face. This strikes her as such a proof of sincerity that she resorts to evoking her duty to her husband. And although the knight argues that taking pity on him would be as much to her spiritual credit as a pilgrimage overseas, she still refuses, and refuses also a ring he offers her.

The inner debate between the lady's inclination and Reason grows so intense that she falls into a kind of distraction. The knight slips the ring on her finger unobserved and hastily takes his leave. Jean Renart does not give names to this knight and lady, the better for them to represent the generalized human problem of evaluating appearances. Underneath the advances and retreats of the conversation, Jean Renart lets us perceive real emotions. The lady is not as indifferent as she appears. When the knight leaves abruptly, she thinks his words must after all have been false. The sight of the ring on her finger is a relief, but then she worries that acceptance of it might make him believe she was easily won. She decides to throw the ring in the well if the knight won't take it back.

He, summoned by the lady's messenger, is sure that his ring has had the desired effect. When, despite his long pleas and protestations, he finds it in his hand again, he is inspired to say he will give it instead to "next to you the one / I love best" (888–89). Here again the lady's reaction tells us her real feelings: she imagines for an instant that she has already been replaced. Such credulity can be explained by intensity of interest; she fears to lose something she really values. When the knight gives the ring to her reflection, she perceives him as a model of graciousness and acknowledges her own feeling of love.

John Stevens writes that the knight's response "seems to crystallize for all time an exquisite moment of courtliness; . . . a gesture of almost quixotic courtesy [that] claims the lady's surrender." [53] It certainly creates a crisis in their elegant, stylized conversation, to which she has to respond. But Jean Renart tells us in the beginning of the *lai* that what the knight suffered because of love was worse than having teeth pulled by a barber. The image strikes us as incongruous because it is so physical, inappropriate to the knight's words but not, in fact, to the nature of his quest. The lady herself has no illusions about this. The knight had boasted that a year and a half would be enough for her to make him worthy of her love. But they are still sitting beside the well, which Jean Renart has told us was not very deep, when, without further talk of "service," he takes her in his arms.

ALL THE ELEMENTS of a love relationship that are cheerfully omitted from *The Reflection* are the substance of *The Chatelaine of Vergi*. Here courtship is in the past, a mutual trust having been long since established, and the couple's physical relationship reflects their real commitment to each other. The *lai* has obvious affinities with *Lanval* and may have been written in response to it. But the chatelaine is a human being, and we can participate in her emotions, whereas we really have no access to those of the *fée*.[54]

Although Lanval, in a moment of inattention, broke his promise, he was ultimately allowed to determine his own fate. The author of *The Chatelaine of Vergi* turns the same biblical plot of Potiphar's wife into an inexorable trap. The commonsensical ways out—the knight could have found a way to tell the lady his dilemma, she could have had enough confidence in him to wait and ask questions—simply do not apply. As soon ask why Othello trusted Iago more than Desdemona. Tragic art gives a sense that things could not be otherwise.[55]

An analysis of the plot shows a series of interconnected betrayals, a formal structure in which two peripheral figures serve as innocent messengers: the little dog, whose presence was a signal for the knight, and the serving girl. The latter was in the room, unseen, when the chatelaine died, crouching beside the bed as if she too were a kind of household pet, unable to intervene. The betrayals are not spontaneous, like Lanval's, but always the result of a decision: the duchess decides to revenge herself on the knight by lying to her husband, the nature of her accusation being such that the knight then decides his best response is to tell his secret to the duke, who in turn decides he should entrust it to his wife, because she tells him that true love (even in marriage) requires perfect faith. Finally, the chatelaine decides she has nothing left to live for, since her lover revealed their secret—and did so, as she believes, for love of the duchess.

The chatelaine's monologue—an invocation to death, a *Liebestod*—seems to break free of this sequence of events. Like Aude, Iseut, and the young princess in *The Two Lovers,* she dies, without violence, for love. But the chatelaine dies because her lover betrayed her. The emphasis is on love, past and present, rather than grief. Lost happiness is evoked without bitterness; the chatelaine forgives the unfaithful knight and asks God to bless him. But in fact, in the temporal world of narrative, she does her lover an injustice. We might admire the chatelaine less, if we did not know she was wrong. As it is, most readers are moved by her words, melodic even within the rigid couplets. They make the cruel mistakes of life inexplicably beautiful.

NOTES

1.   Raymond A. Mc Coy, *The Golden Goddess: Ancient Egyptian Love Lyrics* (Menomonie, Wisconsin: Enchiridion Publications, 1972), 20.

2.   "Pus vezem de novel florir," in *Lyrics of the Troubadours and Trouvères,* ed. and trans. Frederick Goldin (Garden City, N.Y.: Anchor Books, 1973), 36–40.

3.   *Fin' amor* literally means "refined love." William Calin suggests that the term "courtly love," first used by Gaston Paris in 1881, was intended as a "kind of translation of the expression *fin' amor* as used in Provençal and in Old French." "Defense and Illustration of *Fin' Amor,*" in *The Expansions and Transformations of Courtly Literature* (Athens, Georgia: University of Georgia Press, 1980), 34. Peter Dronke gives a more generalized definition of *fin' amor* in his discussion of the troubadour Marcabru: "*Fin' Amors* is all that is true, truly loved or truly loving, in whatever mode, earthly or heavenly, it finds expression; all that is genuinely felt, devoid of treachery or dissembling, calculation or greed or fear." *The Medieval Lyric* (London: Hutchinson University Library, 1968), 210.

4.   In his *Medieval Romance* (New York: Norton, 1973), John Stevens calls attention to this phenomenon in Chaucer's *Troilus and Criseyde,* quoting 1:1076–78 to illustrate "the ennoblement of Troilus, his social improvement (to put it no higher): 'And in the town his manere tho forth

ay / Soo goodly was, and gat hym so in grace, / That ecch hym loved that loked on his face'" (40).

5. Maurice Valency, *In Praise of Love* (New York: Macmillan, 1961), 26.

6. "Mout jauzens me prenc en amar," lines 14–15, translated by Goldin, *Lyrics of the Troubadours*, 43.

7. "Ab la dolchor del temps nouvel," lines 22–24, ibid., 46.

8. Goldin, *Lyrics of the Troubadours*, 14–15.

9. Gilbert Highet, *The Classical Tradition* (New York: Oxford University Press, 1949), 578n. 34. Meg Bogin notes that "the Arab poets had used a similar form of address, variously given as *sidi* or *sayidd*—'my lord'—in their love poems to women." *The Women Troubadours* (New York: Paddington Press Ltd., 1976), 50n.

10. W. T. H. Jackson, *Medieval Literature* (New York: Collier Books, 1966), 97. Highet, *Classical Tradition*, 576n. 12, agrees that this story was invented by Benoît.

11. Highet, *Classical Tradition*, 56.

12. Dronke, *Medieval Lyric*, 86–90.

13. In Bogin's analysis, "The women, unlike the men, do not idealize the relationships they write about, nor do they use the lover and the lady as allegorical figures. The women write about relationships that are immediately recognizable to us; they do not worship men, nor do they seem to want to be adored themselves." *Women Troubadours*, 13.

She notes that the *trobairitz* were a local phenomenon of one generation only: "Certain key factors—their legal heritage, the effect of the Crusades, and their aristocratic birth—converged during their lifetime in a way that set them apart from their mothers and grandmothers and from their contemporaries elsewhere in Europe. . . . Marie de France . . . was virtually alone [among women poets in northern France]" (36).

14. Shulamith Shahar's statement is representative: "It should be recalled that even if this literature reflected a social reality, it was the reality of only a narrow stratum of the female population. . . . And even where noblewomen were concerned, the courtly literature had hardly any social effect. It brought no changes in their standing, either *de jure* or *de facto*." *The Fourth Estate* (London: Methuen, 1983), 163.

15. Suzanne Wemple's study of Frankish society concludes that "compared to women in antiquity and primitive Germanic societies, early medieval women had achieved considerable legal and social rights. . . . The

mutual influence of Germanic and Roman customs in family law and mat-
rimonial arrangements resulted in the amelioration of women's status.
Women in families of Roman descent were no longer treated as perpetual
minors." *Women in Frankish Society* (Philadelphia: University of Pennsylvania
Press, 1981), 189.

By contrast, "a woman under feudalism spent most of her life under the
guardianship of a man—of her father until she married, of her father's lord
if her father died, and of her husband until she was widowed. The lord
pocketed the money of his ward's estate, and she had to marry a man of
his choice or lose her inheritance." Frances and Joseph Gies, *Women in the
Middle Ages* (New York: Harper Perennial, 1978), 27.

16. *Mâle moyen âge* (Paris: Flammarion, 1988), 93. Duby sees this "man's
game" as being played by the *husband,* who reinforces his power over the
young men of his household by offering his wife as the object of their admi-
ration. Their instructress in the civilizing arts by which she might be won,
she is nonetheless inviolable, as the *seigneur's* wife; hence the intensification
and frustration of desire. "By exhibiting his largesse to the point of letting
his lady pretend that she was gradually giving herself, he was able to gain
an ever stronger hold over the young men of his household, to domesticate
them in the proper sense of that term." *Medieval Marriage* (Baltimore: Johns
Hopkins University Press, 1978), 14. Meg Bogin also believes that the
poet's praise of his lady may have been intended primarily to please her husband (*Women Troubadours,* 50–51).

This hidden motivation would not, of course, apply in lyric poems written by a *seigneur,* like Guillaume IX or Thibaut de Champagne, nor is it
reflected in courtly romances. Duby understands the romances as primarily
expressing the aspirations of the *juvenes,* younger sons who sought not a mistress but a wife, that is, property (*The Chivalrous Society* [Berkeley: University of California Press, 1977], chapter 7). The protagonists of Chrétien de
Troyes's *Yvain* and Renaud de Beaujeu's *Le Bel Inconnu* offer examples of such
young men. Of those represented in this collection, Lanval would be closest
to the type.

17. Quoted by Goldin, *Lyrics of the Troubadours,* 5.

18. Shahar writes, "According to many historians this body of work,
more than anything which came before, typified literature written on the
inspiration of women, elevating their image and answering their psychological needs. Recent interpretation of courtly literature, on the other hand,

emphasizes the inner needs of man to which this literature answered. . . . Love in courtly literature is the center of man's life. In order to win the love of his adored lady he must endure all the trials she imposes on him. This conduct was in complete contrast both to the marriage customs of the nobility, . . . and to the status of the married woman, who was subject by law to the authority of her husband. . . . But most important for the image of woman is the fact that in courtly literature she is not seen as a destructive force; in most of the works, love for a woman is a source of inspiration for heroic action and a factor enhancing all the moral traits of the lover." *Fourth Estate,* 161–62.

19. Geoffrey of Monmouth, *History of the Kings of Britain,* trans. Sebastian Evans and Charles Dunn (New York: E. P. Dutton, 1958), 202.

20. Stevens, *Medieval Romance,* 38.

21. A verse translation is Harriet Spiegel, ed. and trans., *Fables* (Toronto: University of Toronto Press, 1987).

22. *Guigemar,* line 3, as quoted by Glyn S. Burgess, *Marie de France: Text and Context* (Athens: The University of Georgia Press, 1987), 74.

23. Stevens, *Medieval Romance,* 239. It is uncertain whether Marie considered herself to be writing *lais* or whether in using this word she refers to her sources. In any event, her own form of narrative verse has come to be called a *lai.*

24. Joan Ferrante, *Woman as Image in Medieval Literature* (New York: Columbia University Press, 1975), 97.

25. Jean Renart, *L'Escoufle* (Paris: Droz, 1974), line 5509.

26. René Ernst Victor Stuip, ed., *La Chastelaine de Vergi* (The Hague: Mouton, 1970), 65. A *chastelaine* was the wife of the lord of a castle.

27. Jean Frappier, *Chrétien de Troyes* (Paris: Hatier, 1968), 62–68.

28. Highet, *Classical Tradition,* 78.

29. René Girard suggests that she was lynched, in *Violence and the Sacred,* quoted by Patricia Klindienst Joplin, "The Voice of the Shuttle Is Ours," *Stanford Literary Review* 1 (spring 1984): 44n. 34.

30. Ibid., 50.

31. In the Old French the heroine's name is Philomena, a spelling already found in the Ovid manuscripts that Chrétien would have used. Nancy A. Jones analyzes the elements of the name in Old French, showing how it "encapsulates an action": *fil* (thread; son), *fille* (daughter), *phil*

(Greek *philia,* or love), and *mena,* from *mener* (to lead)—a verb that "virtually guides the plot," as Philomena guides the thread. Jones cites numerous examples to show the predominance of this verb, noting also the extraordinary rhyme: ". . . Philomena / . . . menee l'an a" (Old French lines 729–30). "The Daughter's Text and the Thread of Lineage in the Old French *Philomena,*" unpublished article, 17–25.

32. Geoffrey Hartman, "The Voice of the Shuttle: Language from the Point of View of Literature," in *Beyond Formalism: Literary Essays 1958–70* (New Haven: Yale University Press, 1970), 337; quoted by Joplin, "Voice of the Shuttle," 25. "The voice of the shuttle," Joplin notes, is a phrase from Sophocles' lost play, apparently called *Tereus,* quoted by Aristotle (*Poetics* 16.4).

33. E. Jane Burns points out that the list of Philomena's accomplishments "ends, significantly, with a reference to her accomplished speech." *Bodytalk* (Philadelphia: University of Pennsylvania Press, 1993), 123.

34. Burns refers to Philomena's father as "the ogling Pandion" (*Bodytalk,* 26–27).

35. Burns comments on this undervaluing of women's *savoir* and on the crucial part played by the old woman's skill in Philomena's self-liberation (*Bodytalk,* 132).

36. In Kathryn Gravdal's view, "The fictional law Chrétien invents, invokes, and then 'puts aside' actually deals with incestuous adultery. But the medieval poet quickly shifts our attention away from that fact. Repeating the word *loi* four times, and dwelling on the lexicon of pleasure . . . , Chrétien allows the audience to infer that Tereus' rape of Philomena was justifiable." *Ravishing Maidens* (Philadelphia: University of Pennsylvania Press, 1991), 63. It is also possible, and fully compatible with his understated style, that Chrétien invented this "law" to produce just the opposite effect.

37. Raymond Cormier argues that "on peut déceler une douleur sincère derrière les larmes de Térée" (one can detect a sincere sadness behind Tereus's tears). "Térée, le pêcheur fatal dans *Philomena,*" *Dalhousie French Studies* 24 (spring–summer 1993): 1–9; my translation.

38. Frappier comments on this statement, "N'est pas amors de forsener" (Old French line 486): "Cette maxime s'accorde au mieux avec la doctrine que les romans de Chrétien ne cesseront de défendre" (This maxim is in

total agreement with the doctrine that will be argued in all of Chrétien's romances). *Chrétien de Troyes,* 68; my translation.

39. Ovid, *The Metamorphoses,* trans. Horace Gregory (New York: Viking, 1958), 169. Robert Cargo may well be right when he suggests that Ovid's earlier connection between Philomela and the woodlands, "'If I am shut up in these woods, I will fill the woods with my story and move the very rocks to pity' [lines 546–47], . . . establishes the specific Philomena-nightingale metamorphosis." "Marie de France *Le Laüstic* and Ovid's *Metamorphoses,*" *Comparative Literature* 18 (1966): 163n. 2; Cargo's translation. In turning Philomena into a nightingale Chrétien may have been responding to this passage, or he may have had an additional source.

40. As Nicole Loraux observes, "She [Procne] weeps both for her loss and for having committed the act which caused that loss." "The Mourning of the Nightingale," *Pequod* 35 (1993): 34.

41. Wendy Pfeffer indicates, based on the use of *oci* for the nightingale's cry in the work of a later poet, a date for *Philomena* before 1245. *The Change of Philomel: The Nightingale in Medieval Literature* (New York: Peter Lang, 1985), 137.

42. Nancy Vine Durling, "The Knot, the Belt, and the Making of *Guigemar,*" *Assays* 6 (1991): 34. Durling interprets the verb *estreindre* in line 240 as "embrace" and convincingly argues that the reference is to Ovid's *Ars amatoria* (ibid., 50n. 13).

43. Fowles's foreword to Robert Hanning and Joan Ferrante's translation, *The Lais of Marie de France* (New York: E. P. Dutton, 1978), xi; Burgess, *Marie de France,* 109–10; Jacques Ribard, "Le Lai du *Laüstic*: structure et signification," *Moyen âge* 76 (1970): 273–74.

44. Paula Clifford, *Marie de France: Lais* (London: Grant and Cutler Ltd., 1982), 71.

45. Hanning and Ferrante, trans., *Lais,* 136.

46. Ibid., 133–36.

47. See Michelle A. Freeman, "Marie de France's Poetics of Silence: The Implications for a Feminine *Translatio,*" *PMLA* 99 (1984): 871. Along with most critics, Freeman assumes the meaning is "his name," agreeing with Frappier that what was written was *only* that (872). Her article gives a summary of the varying opinions regarding the "message" (872–74). Freeman's

sensitive analysis of the *lais* interprets the lack of clarity on such matters as part of Marie's "poetics of silence."

48. Ibid., 874.

49. In Jean-Claude Aubailly's Jungian analysis of *Lanval,* the Other World is understood as the unconscious. The young knight does not pass over the boundary but abandons himself instead to a kind of dream. The resulting confrontation with the *fée,* the archetypal Anima, enriches his life in society, but he finds no way to unite the source of his joy and the world of reality. *La Fée et le chevalier* (Paris: Honoré Champion, 1986), 81–82, 88–89.

50. Hanning and Ferrante remark that "perhaps, in some way, his behavior to the second [lord] justifies the way the first behaved toward him" (*Lais,* 232). By contrast Philippe Ménard, summing up his view of Eliduc's character, calls him "notre semblable" (so much like us) and asks, "Comment en vouloir au sympathique Eliduc, si humain, trop humain?" (How can we hold this against our dear Eliduc, so human, too human?). *Les Lais de Marie de France* (Paris: Presses Universitaires de France, 1979), 121.

51. Marie obviously does not agree with the "famous decision" recorded by Andreas, chaplain to Marie de Champagne, to the effect that if a woman marries her lover, their love is at an end (Andreas Capellanus, *The Art of Courtly Love,* trans. John Jay Parry [New York: Norton, 1969], 175). Her *Milun* also ends with a marriage of love, and *Guigemar* does (presumably) as well.

52. Patricia Terry, "Hearing and Seeing in the Works of Jean Renart: What Is Believing?" *Romance Languages Annual* 4 (1993): 157 et passim.

53. Stevens, *Medieval Romance,* 192.

54. A. Maraud, "Le Lai de *Lanval* et *La Chastelaine de Vergi*: la structure narrative," *Romania* 93 (1972): 433–59 passim. Maraud points out this distinction on p. 457; the observations that follow owe much to his article.

55. Paul Zumthor sees this inevitability as a feature of the lyric poetry of love, like the song quoted in lines 295–302 of the text, in which the sentiments and acts of the lovers exist in a universe apart. *Langue, texte, énigme* (Paris: Seuil, 1975), 229.

PHILOMENA

ADAPTED FROM OVID'S *METAMORPHOSES*, BOOK 6

Chrétien de Troyes

In Athens, Pandion ruled the state,
A generous, courtly potentate.
Of all in life that gave him pleasure,
His daughters were his greatest treasure: 4
Philomena, the younger one,
And Procne, whose hand had just been won.
Her father heard with much good grace
A proposal from the king of Thrace.   8
What made him glad of such a plan?*
He thought he'd found a worthy man,
A king! A king? It is a shame
To call him that. The tyrant's name   12
Was Tereus. Without debate,
Pandion set the wedding date.
With evil omens they were wed:
Hymen, the god who should have led   16
The ceremonies, did not come;
The chanting priests were as if struck dumb;
No one at all seemed to rejoice.
Procne and Tereus heard the voice   20
Of an owl screeching near their room
All night, and other portents of doom
Were there: barn owl, cuckoo, crow—
Not a good sign. These omens show   24
There'll be no way to find relief
From hardship that must come, and grief.
In an evil hour they were wed:

Through the palace where they lay in bed,   28
Demons flew with Tesiphone
And Atropos, horrors waiting to be.*
Tereus did not choose to stay
After the wedding; he sailed away,   32
Back to Thrace with his noble wife,
His queen. There she would live her life.
And there was born to them a son—
Better by far if they'd had none!   36
Throughout the kingdom there was joy
Upon the birth of the royal boy,
And each year an extravagant
Festival, as for Tervagant,*   40
Was held by Tereus's decree.
So well did the baby thrive that he
Was beautiful by the age of five.
Alas! He would not stay alive   44
Much longer! Itis was his name.
Soon I will tell you what became
Of this child, how he met his fate,
But first I've something else to relate.   48
Procne had, by my reckoning,
Been more than five years with the king,
And she was longing to see her sister,
Philomena; she truly missed her.   52
For quite some time she did not mention
Anything of her intention—
She was reluctant, lest it grieve
Her husband that she wished to leave.   56
At last she could not hold her peace;
She said she wanted to go to Greece,
Asking for the king's permission
To visit her sister, on condition   60
That she would not be long away.

If he refused, she would obey
But ask that he go in her place
And bring Philomena back to Thrace.   64
He answered that Procne must remain
At home, that she must not complain,
Since he, whatever the trip required,
Was willing to do as she desired.   68
And so, as Tereus decreed,
All the provisions he would need
Were quickly readied for the trip,
The mast and sails put on each ship.   72
Soon it was done. He went on board,
And many with him. Procne implored
Her husband to bring her sister back
As soon as he could. The sails were slack,   76
But at sea they filled, the ropes strained tight,
And all day long and all the night,
Steering by the stars, they sailed.
Good winds and peaceful seas prevailed,   80
Alas! On a straight course they steered—
If only something had interfered!
Fate would have shown a kinder face,
Had Procne kept the king in Thrace;   84
Great sorrow came because he went.
Quickly a messenger was sent
To give King Pandion the report
That ships had come into his port.   88
As soon as the king was made aware
That his own son-in-law was there,
Wanting to see him, he didn't waste
A moment. Pandion left in haste,   92
Met Tereus at the landing place,
And kissed his eyes and mouth and face
In joyful greeting. That being done,

He saluted all the rest as one   96
And led them toward his city. The king
Was eager to know everything
About his daughter and the boy.
Were they happy? Did they enjoy   100
Good health? All at home was well,
Tereus was quick to tell,
And both sent him their love from Thrace.
Then he began to state his case,   104
Explaining what his visit meant:
"And yet your daughter is not content,
Sire; it has been too long a time
Since she's seen Philomena. I'm   108
Here as Procne's messenger,
And I hope, as you are fond of her,
That you will listen to her plea
And send Philomena home with me.   112
I know you will sorely feel the lack,
And will want her to come quickly back—
Too long it would seem were she to stay
Just one hour or a single day—   116
And so I solemnly do swear
That as soon as winds are blowing fair
To speed her safely on her way,
I will make sure she does not stay;   120
I'll bring her back. But I've been treated
Badly when I've not yet been greeted
By your daughter; that's a sad surprise."
And suddenly, there before his eyes   124
Stood Philomena, her hair undone—
She didn't look like a cloistered nun!
She had come quickly from inside.
Greater writers than I have tried   128
To portray such beauty. I will need

A miracle or I won't succeed.
To tell of her loveliness and grace,
Her fair body, her radiant face,   132
Would take more skill than that of Plato,
Or of Homer, or of Cato,*
Who for their wisdom were acclaimed;
So I don't have to feel ashamed   136
If I can't manage it in this work.
I'll do my best, and I will not shirk.
Now I've begun, I won't be deterred;
For what I say, try to take my word.   140
The beauty of her head will be told
First of all: like the purest gold
Gleaming bright was her lovely hair.
God had fashioned her so fair   144
That I think had Nature undertaken
Improvement, she'd have been mistaken.
Her unlined forehead was broad and white;
Rivaling jewels, her eyes were bright;   148
Her wide-spaced brows were finely made,
Needing no artificial aid.
Long and straight was her perfect nose;
Her cheeks mingled lilies and the rose.   152
Her lips were red enough: they vied
With scarlet samite freshly dyed;
Her mouth was full and made for mirth.
Spice, balm, and incense are not worth   156
The fragrance of her breathing. All
Her teeth were white, closely spaced, and small.
Her chin and neck, her lovely throat,
Were whiter than an ermine's coat;   160
Her tiny breasts were like a pair
Of little apples. White and fair,
Her hands were long to the fingertips;

Her waist slender, low-set her hips;   164
And, to summarize, the rest,
In all its aspects, was the best
Ever seen by human eyes,
For Nature in this enterprise   168
Had really worked as hard as she could.*
Philomena understood
So many things that I can swear
She was as wise as she was fair,   172
Truly learned. She knew all sorts
Of entertaining games and sports—
More than the men best known to us,
Like Tristan or Apollonius.*   176
Both chess and backgammon she could play,
"Six and Ace" from an earlier day,
And "Buffet and Battle." She was adored*
And wooed by many a noble lord,   180
She was such delightful company.
She was excellent at falconry,
With peregrine and sparrow hawk
And even lanners, though they balk;*   184
Falcons, tercels, goshawks—all three
She brought through their molts. She loved to be*
Out hawking close to a river's shore
Or in the field. Yet no one had more   188
Talent for working cloth dyed rich
Crimson; she had the skill to stitch
Figured silk or fine brocade
And ghostly Hellequins portrayed   192
In beautifully colored thread.*
Skilled in language too, well-read,
The maiden could write both verse and prose,
And she could perform, as she chose,   196
Music on psaltery or lyre.

Who has the art it would require
To tell all her talents? She could play
The *vielle* to accompany a *lai*—*   200
There wasn't a tune she did not know—
And when she talked her words were so
Full of wisdom, she could teach
Without a book, just through her speech.   204
And now, her face rosy and bright,
She came toward her father, in a samite
Tunic that was tightly laced.
From the moment Tereus embraced   208
And greeted her, and they had kissed,
He was quite unable to resist
Her beauty: it was like a dart
That struck him deep within the heart.   212
Evil love that came unbidden
Caused him to hope for things forbidden,
Desires terrible and mad.
Evil love? Yes! Love can be bad;   216
Vilely indeed was he inspired
When his wife's sister he desired.
Had his own sister been the attraction,
He could have taken any action.   220
Pagans to all desires could yield;
Their joys could remain quite unconcealed,
A god having long since decreed—
So it was established in their creed—   224
That love of a sister was permitted.
Tereus would have been acquitted—
Because, by law, it was his right
To take her for his heart's delight—   228
If someone brought it to a trial.
No matter how scandalous and vile
His pleasures were, they could not say

He had done wrong in any way.   232
But that's enough about pagan law!*
Who, among humans, ever saw
Any power over Love's prevail?
In an evil hour did Tereus sail   236
To take Philomena out of Greece.
Now Love has put an end to peace;
He has been tricked and brought to shame,
His heart on fire with that flame   240
That is so easily ignited.
Tereus, utterly delighted
To hold the maiden in his embrace,
Makes a speech that is full of grace: 244
"My dear, I'm your sister's messenger.
I bring you fondest greetings from her.
She misses you. She is quite bereft;
It's been such a long time since she left.   248
If she could see you, she'd rejoice.
And to her plea I add my voice,
For what it may be worth; if my prayer
Were answered, you would soon be there.   252
This is all that Procne prays for:
To hold you in her arms once more.
And, in truth, she herself would be
Here with you now, had she been free.   256
Her great desire was to come in quest
Of you on her own, but that request
I refused. I would not let her depart,
In spite of the hunger in her heart;   260
I forced her to stay. Your sister seeks
To have you with her for just two weeks.
I hope I've not journeyed uselessly!
If you ask the king, he must agree   264
That it would be only fair and right

To let you go and bring delight
To your sister in that distant place.
She let me know, when I left Thrace, 268
That if I failed in my mission here,
She would no longer hold me dear.
I'd rather be feeble, bald, and old
Than have her love for me turn cold! 272
Tell your father that, by his grace,
You'd like to come with me to Thrace."
But to this, Philomena replies,
Being, as I have said, most wise: 276
"Sire, how could any words I say
Compare to yours? If you want to sway*
My father, you would have more chance
If you spoke first—at least in France 280
That is the custom. Those who crave
Boons, if they're competent and brave,
Should try to achieve their own desires,
Whatever effort this requires! 284
After that, if they don't succeed,
Another person may intercede."
"Demoiselle, that may all be true,
But one small point eluded you; 288
You have forgotten just one thing:
Perhaps I've already asked the king."
"Indeed! That proves how little wit
I have—I never thought of it! 292
I should have found out right away.
Now tell me, what did you really say
To my lord? How much did you explain?
Was your intention very plain?" 296
"Demoiselle, I thought it best
To be discreet with my request
And only mention it in passing."

"What did he reply?" "The king   300
Said nothing." "Then it's no loss
If that response receives no gloss.
It's clear that Procne will have to wait
For months. I know the king would hate   304
To grant permission for what you ask;
Yours is a most ungrateful task."
"He won't want to?" "I don't think so."
"What makes you believe that?" "I just know,   308
Because he preferred not to reply."
"There may be another reason why.
Nothing he said was negative;
To do as we ask could even give   312
Him pleasure. At least he heard me out,
And didn't seem distressed about
My plan. For as experience teaches,
Generous men do not make speeches."   316
"That's not a saying I believe;
We still don't know if he'll give me leave
Or refuse to let me visit Thrace."
Then Tereus was face-to-face   320
With Pandion to try once more:
"Sire, I've done what I came here for.
I've tried my very best to present
The message that your daughter sent.   324
If all the men on earth combine
To make a request of you, still mine,
I believe, over that one should prevail.
At least I'm sure you'd never fail   328
In the generosity that is due
Your daughters. What you might not do
For me, I know you could not refuse
Either of them, and both now use   332
My voice. They want me to intercede

With you; on their behalf I'll plead
Until Philomena is allowed
To come to Thrace." Pandion bowed   336
His head and leaned it on his hand.
To yield to Tereus's demand
Was not at all what he desired,
But even so, he was required   340
To answer. "You don't have to be told,
My friend, that I would never withhold
Anything that you asked me for—
You'd not speak twice, much less implore!   344
But if you had a chance of seeing
My daughter's care for my well-being,
You wouldn't ask for such a boon.
Without my daughter, very soon   348
Despair would overwhelm my heart.
In just one day I'd have to start
Leaning on crutches and a cane,
And that's the way I would remain   352
Forever. So, if you don't mind,
We'll set aside your request and find
An agreed-upon but later date."
"Later?" "Yes." "How long must we wait?"   356
"Only as long as there's life in me.
It must be easy enough to see
That I'm so very weak and old
My days on earth are nearly all told.   360
Abraham lived fewer years than I;
I've passed both Jacob and Esau by
I have accumulated treasure,
But nothing gives me any pleasure   364
Except my daughter. I still live
Because of the comfort she can give;
That's all I have to sustain me now.

My time will be short if I allow   368
Philomena to leave. If you insist
On taking her, I won't exist
More than a little while. The way,
Evening and morning, night and day,   372
She is always watching over me—
If I could only make you see
What, if I lost her, I would lose!
She dresses me, puts on my shoes;   376
When I get up my daughter is there,
And when I go to bed. She takes care
Of all my needs; by her command,
No one else may even lend a hand.   380
It's thanks to her love that I'm still here.
I beg you, if you hold me dear,
From this request let me be excused."
Tereus felt himself abused.   384
He had heard nothing to his taste,
And felt his journey had been a waste.
Ill at ease and in great distress,
With nothing to do, no thought to express,   388
He looked defeated, and he sighed
As if it hurt him to have tried
To impose his will and then to fail.
Woe should his mad desire prevail!   392
He stood there saying not a word,
Only his heartfelt groans were heard.
Insanity overcame good sense.
Insanity? Rather, the immense   396
Power of Love which conquers, destroys,
And then from time to time enjoys
Quickly turning things around,
Raising the vanquished from the ground.   400
"Does Love really have such might

That she lets the loser win the fight?"*
"Yes! And those who complain and groan,
Make sure Love's prowess is well known,   404
And so do those who serve her well.
I have arguments to dispel
All doubt: on Love there's no depending;
Her fickleness is never-ending.   408
Her faithful friends may fall from grace;
Others arrive to take their place,
And they're all treated just the same."
"Then I think you were wrong to claim   412
That Love is fickle, since she bestows
The same gifts on all." "That just shows
Love to be really treacherous.
Don't you think every one of us   416
Would agree that even here on earth
Rewards should go to greater worth?
But I understand why Love chooses
The worst she knows, and then refuses   420
Very much better candidates.
The reason why she so frustrates
The deserving is she has no test
To determine which are really best."   424
"But what about her intelligence?"
"She's wise, but it's her preference
To pay no respect to any facts.
Following her will, she acts.   428
Love is more shifting than the breezes;
False, she'll say anything she pleases.
Her promises are most impressive,
But what she gives is not excessive.   432
She does no harm except to those
Who, pledging their faith to her, chose
To serve her only, became her slaves.

They cannot please her; she behaves   436
More cruelly the more they show
Obedience. No pain or woe
Will ever free them. There can't be
True love without anxiety,   440
And one will always be Love's debtor,
Because one can always love still better.
Love goes her way with no explaining.
Lovers who are the most complaining   444
Are those who are the hardest hit,
Receiving from Love no benefit,
No joy or solace; cure or curse
Love, and you only make it worse.   448
Some think that if they just obey,
They'll have a chance to break away,
But they're more closely bound than ever."
So Tereus, had he been clever,   452
Would have gone back alone to Thrace.
But Philomena's charms, her grace,
Her beauty, her surpassing skill,
Convince him he has to have his will   456
Or surely he will go insane.
He has no power to abstain.*
What then? What strategy to try?
He embraces her, then gives a sigh   460
And weeps, despairing of that hour
When he would have her in his power.
By the evil one who takes no rest,
The Devil, he is so possessed   464
That in his secret heart he knows
He'll bring his visit to a close
Another way, if he can't succeed
By persuasion: force will meet his need.   468
He might steal the girl away by night,

Although he came with only slight
Company; then he hesitates,
Thinking how that could fail, and waits   472
As his hopes rapidly diminish—
Why start what he could never finish?
It seems much better to retreat
Than go on to such a sure defeat.   476
And indeed it would be shameful, vile
Madness to storm the city while
Its people were asleep in bed;
Those from Thrace would soon be dead!   480
"I must say I find it very strange
That Reason had the power to change
Tereus's mind about the schemes
He contemplated. To me it seems   484
He was too far gone for her to teach."
"Why's that?" "What influence can reach
A man obsessed by something more
Than love?" "It's not love?" "You take love for   488
Crime, betrayal? Is going insane
A sign of it? To me it's plain
That no true lover would you find,
Like Tereus, going out of his mind.   492
Now deeper into madness lies
His only way. It's a great surprise
That Reason still could make an appeal."
"Did it?" Tereus began to feel   496
His foul plan should be set aside,
At least until he'd once more tried
To find arguments that would succeed.
Once again, he went to plead   500
With Pandion: "Sire, I can see
There's not very much you'd do for me,
When you refuse this small request.

I've spent much time on a useless quest;   504
I cannot seem to achieve my aim,
And I'm very sorry that I came.
There's little point in vain regret.
All I have left to do is set   508
My course, go home the way I came,
Feeling that I deserve the name
Of fool. Would I'd never seen your face!
Would that I'd never sailed from Thrace!   512
The fact your daughter's of so much use
Provides you with a fine excuse!
If that's why I have toiled in vain,
Traveled so long and far to gain   516
Nothing, it really isn't fair.
Surely you could afford to spare
Your daughter just three days or four,
When there are servants by the score,   520
Maidens and men, in your employ!
You could let Philomena enjoy
At least a little time with Procne,
Who sent me here. Why not agree?   524
It doesn't seem a lot to ask.
If I don't carry out my task,
My regret will be more than double—
First, there's my lost time and trouble;   528
But I put something else above
Even that: I'll have failed my love,
Said Procne, and that if she must lack
Her sister, I need not come back.   532
If, as it seems, I haven't won
My case, I'll also lose my son,
And even more I'll mourn my wife,
Exiled as I shall be for life.   536
That's why you see me shedding tears—

It's terrible to have such fears
Because this small thing you won't allow.
Let me take her, my lord! I vow   540
That within two weeks you'll see her here,
In perfect health and full of cheer.
You'll have a hostage—my good name;
As witnesses, the gods who claim   544
My service. You should not be loath
To trust me on my solemn oath."
How skilled he was at telling lies!
Pandion did not realize   548
That false was everything he heard.
The king took Tereus at his word
Because of all the tears he shed.
The wild, impassioned things he said   552
Seemed, beyond all doubt, sincere;
He pleaded for those whom he held dear.
Such was the wicked tyrant's skill,
His fervent promise to fulfill   556
The sacred, binding oaths he swore,
That it wasn't very long before
The king couldn't help but sympathize.
Tears began to flow from his eyes,   560
And soon the two men wept together;
Indeed, I cannot tell you whether
The tears one shed were more impressive.
Who would consider it excessive   564
In an old man if he's quick to cry?
"My friend," he said, "by the faith that I
Must have, when your oath binds what you say,
I'll let you take my daughter away   568
Tomorrow. I'll leave her in your hands.
Treat her the way that honor demands,
Never forgetting how I grieve

And have only given her short leave.   572
My tears will flow when you depart;
Nothing will bring joy to my heart
Until she's once again in my arms.
Be very sure that nothing harms   576
My daughter. If you should be late,
My love for you will turn to hate.
Be very sure you don't forget this."
Tereus said, "You have my promise,   580
Sire, there is no need to say more.
The longer we stay here on shore,
The longer before I sail and then
Bring Philomena back again."   584
So the conversation ended
Just as Tereus intended.
Pandion agreed to everything.
Then, to please his guest, the king   588
Ordered his servants to begin
Right away bringing tables in.*
His high officials were on hand,
Under the seneschal's command,   592
With bakers and those in charge of wine,
Making sure the service would be fine.
Those who prepared the meat and fish
Took special care with every dish.   596
Every person who was able
Helped at least to set a table
Or to bring the water guests require
To wash their hands. Not a single squire   600
Or well-trained boy was hanging back;
In no way was the service slack.
The entire household showed great zeal.
But nothing they offered could appeal   604
To Tereus, not in the mood

For any kind of drink or food;
His nourishment was just to stare
At Philomena sitting there   608
Right next to him. Her lovely face,
Her fine body's youthful grace—
These were the only things that mattered.
He served her all he could, and flattered,   612
Trying in every way to charm.
No one there could have guessed the harm
He'd do the maiden when at last
He had his chance. A long time passed   616
While they dined, and Tereus was glad
Of every moment that he had
To enjoy her beauty. Just the same,
He couldn't wait till the time came   620
To carry out his vile intention.
Meanwhile, he gave scant attention
To peacock or to swan or pheasant,
To wine the other guests found pleasant,   624
To anything at the royal feast
But Philomena. Slowly decreased
The appetites of those who dined;
Then they left the table to find   628
Servants with silver bowls who poured
Water for every noble lord,
So he could wash and dry his hands.
That accomplished, no one stands;   632
Each joins the others who relax
On couches. The talk can now be lax.
They say whatever comes to mind,
Wise or foolish—every kind   636
Of conversation, even crazy.
The servants, meanwhile, are not lazy,
But make beds ready for the night.

The thought of rest brings no delight   640
To Tereus—it is not sleep
He longs for; he'd prefer to keep
The maiden company, confiding
The feelings he has long been hiding.   644
"What? Do you mean she didn't know?"
"Do you think she'd have agreed to go
Had she realized his secret aim
Was to do her harm and bring her shame?"   648
For the other guests, the time passed
Agreeably until at last
They sought their well-made beds and slept.
But Tereus stayed awake; he kept   652
Tossing and turning. First he tried
The width of his bed, then the long side;
Got up many times; lay down again
With his eyes wide open. The other men,   656
Warm in their comfortable beds,
Did not so much as turn their heads,
Being completely unaware
That a madman lay among them there,   660
Ranting, raving because the night
Was taking so long to yield to light.
When he heard a horn call from the tower
Announcing the first morning hour,   664
Thirty marks of gold as a present
Wouldn't have seemed to him so pleasant.
He quickly ordered all his crew
To get up—there was a lot to do,   668
Because very soon they'd be departing.
Pandion learned that they were starting
The day; they'd want to leave before long.
Although he might have thought it wrong   672
And had a great desire to heed

His fears, he knew that, having agreed,
He must let his daughter go to Thrace.
And she was more than willing; no trace 676
Of apprehension marred her joy.
Thus what we expect to enjoy
Sometimes turns out to be ill-fated.
Philomena was quite elated. 680
She thought she'd have a pleasant sail,
Good winds would certainly prevail
To bring her there and safely back.
She didn't suffer from a lack 684
Of prudence; how could she understand
The horror Tereus had planned?
Who could anticipate such deeds?
And so the tyrant's plan succeeds. 688
They started toward the ship, escorted
By Pandion, who still exhorted
Tereus to keep remembering
The promise he had made to bring 692
Philomena back, and that he'd vowed
Not to exceed the time allowed.
To her the king said, "Oh, my dear!
Do not forget that I am here, 696
Longing for your return. Don't stay
Too long! Don't be too long away!
You—my well-being, my delight,
My joy—I must have you in my sight, 700
Or as long as we remain apart,
Live without comfort for my heart.
Dear daughter, come home soon, and then
I will know happiness again." 704
These words he endlessly repeated,
Embraced her, kissed her, and entreated.
Each time she turned to go on board,

He called her back to him, implored.   708
At last, since nothing could be done,
He commended her to the very one
Who would betray him; unaware,
He gave his sheep to the wolf's good care!   712
To such a shepherd gave his consent!
She's lost, if the tyrant won't repent,
Give up his vile insanity,
But that, it seems, is not to be: 716
All Tereus can think about
Is when he'll be able to start out.
Pandion weeps when at last he must
Say farewell, with a kiss of trust   720
To his vile son-in-law, whose mind
Is all intent on evil, blind
To everything but his own desires.
And now he has all that he requires,   724
With the maiden wholly in his hands.
Wind fills the sails as Pandion stands
Weeping. The ship is moving fast.
Rightly he weeps, for that's the last   728
Of his poor daughter he'll ever see.
He doesn't know there will never be
A homecoming for her; very near,
Now, is the worst that he could fear.   732
The tyrant, totally obsessed,
Brought her to a house he possessed,
An isolated, lonely place
In the tale of Chrétien li Gois.*   736
Far from everything it stood,
Hidden away deep in a wood.
There were no people close at hand,
No towns, no cultivated land,   740
No roads, not even paths led there.

Philomena was kept unaware
That anything could be the matter
By Tereus's cheerful chatter, 744
And even finding herself alone
Inside with him, could not have known,
Although they were far from humankind,
The evil that he had in mind. 748
He draws her close with his right arm.
She doesn't think she'll come to harm,
Doesn't know what his move implies—
Too innocent to realize, 752
Despite his amorous embraces,
The real danger that she faces.
Whenever a thief need have no fear
That anything can interfere, 756
And he is free to do his worst,
He won't care which foot he puts first.
There's joy for him in wicked deeds;
If he has the daring that it needs, 760
Nothing can stop him. In the eyes
Of honorable men, loyal, wise,
Such crimes would be repugnant, wild.
But nothing in Tereus was mild 764
Or noble. Overwhelmingly strong
Was the impulse in him to do wrong.
At any cost, his heart required
That he obtain all he desired, 768
Whatever evil that involved.
Yet, courteously, he resolved
To see if he could win her heart
By wooing her, and not just start 772
Using his strength as an argument:
"I love you. I hope that you'll consent,
Beautiful one, to rejoice my heart.

But, so we won't soon have to part,   776
We must share our love in secret, here."
"Why is that, my lord? I hold you dear,
As indeed I should; why do you speak
Of concealing it? But if you seek   780
Unlawful love, there's no more to say."
"Agreed, if I can have my way!
So fervently do I admire
Your charms, so intense is my desire—   784
Please understand that have you I must!"
"Surely you would not abuse my trust,
My lord—you could not be so vile!
God forbid that you love me while   788
My sister is your lawful wife!
Don't betray her! Bring no strife
Among us! Never will I agree
To give Procne cause for jealousy.   792
I'll never do what she'd grieve to hear!"
"Oh, won't you?" "No!" "But you are here
To do exactly as I choose!
Nothing I ask can you refuse,   796
Like it or not. You can't prevent
My accomplishing my heart's intent."
"You can't really mean that!" "Here and now,
I am resolved to show you how!   800
And even if this place has spies,
I'm not concerned about prying eyes!"
He seizes her, and she resists,
Crying out as she turns and twists,   804
Frantic, so overwhelmed with fears
She is close to death. Color appears,
Flushing her face; then she turns pale
From rage and pain as her struggles fail,   808
And in anguish she must understand

That she had left her native land
In an evil hour for this disgrace.
"Traitor!" she cries, "what wicked race   812
Do you come from? Traitor! Evil man!
Tell me, traitor, what is your plan?
Why have you brought me here by guile?
Accursed traitor! Loathsome, vile!   816
Is there nothing, traitor, you respect?
You made a promise to protect
My honor, traitor! Solemnly swore
To bring me, safe and sound, once more   820
To my home, to my father, the king,
Who believed—traitor!—everything
You told him, putting aside his fears
Because he saw you shedding tears   824
And because he heard your sacred vow
To all your gods. Where are they now,
Those gods? Do you not see any need
For remembering your holy creed?   828
What happened to the tears that streamed
From your eyes, and to my father seemed
Proof of your honesty. I too
Saw you weeping and never knew,   832
Alas, that it was all deceit.
What is it makes you lie and cheat?
Traitor! You must be out of your mind!
But even now you still could find   836
A way to redeem yourself. There's time,
Even now, to renounce this crime
And repent before it is too late!"*
So she tried to avert her fate,   840
Poor maiden, but that was not to be.
The tyrant cared nothing for her plea
Or for repentance. Then and there,

Tereus brought all his strength to bear   844
Against her; and she fought until
He took his pleasure, though she fought still.
It's truly said: an evil deed
Another evil is bound to breed,   848
Feeding the first. Soon it will grow
And multiply; its foul source will show.
Tereus found, ready at hand,
A small, sharp knife, as if he'd planned   852
A crime to hide the first. He explained
He must make sure she never complained,
Never revealed to anyone
Her shame, the deed that he had done.   856
Just one stroke, and she would lose
Her tongue, and then what could she use
To tell of his betrayal? The act
Followed; seizing her tongue, he hacked   860
Almost half of it out. A foul crime
He thus committed a second time.
And then the tyrant left her there,
Locked in the house, where her despair,   864
Her weeping and the sounds she made,
Would not be heard. The men who stayed
Waiting nearby knew what their lord
Had done, but they could not afford   868
To say a word, because of fear;
It wasn't that they held him dear.
But Tereus did a foolish thing:
To guard Philomena, the king   872
Brought a peasant woman who, instead
Of farming, lived by spinning thread
And weaving cloth. Her daughter stayed
With her, being taught the trade.   876
And now the old woman, bidden

To keep Philomena hidden,
Had many questions. Most unwise
Was Tereus in his replies.   880
When the woman had no more to ask,
Tereus said it would be her task
To stay, without exception, near
Philomena; nothing must interfere.   884
Whatever was needed or desired,
Her constant presence would be required.
She swore to it convincingly;
Tereus felt he need not be   888
A moment longer in that place,
So he returned to his home in Thrace.
Procne had not the slightest doubt
Her husband would not come back without   892
Her sister. Great was the joy she had
In her heart, but she would not be glad
For very long. They were all there,
Her husband and his lords, but where   896
Was the one with whom she would rejoice?
Nothing she heard, no other voice,
Was welcome; she spoke no words of cheer,
"God save you" or "I'm glad you're here."   900
Scarcely waiting to be greeted,
Procne fearfully entreated,
"Why didn't Philomena come?
Where is she? Can't you give me some   904
Reason for this strange delaying?
Where did you leave her? Where's she staying?
Why didn't she come here instead?"
The cruel traitor bowed his head   908
And made his whole appearance suggest
That he was exceedingly depressed.
He gave an artificial sigh,

The better to conceal the lie   912
With which he planned to deceive his wife.
"My lady," he said, "in this sad life
We have to be resigned about
The things that we must do without."   916
"True, and your saying so makes me fear
That my sister won't be coming here."
"She won't; that cannot be denied."
"But what made Philomena decide   920
Against it?" "Of that I will not speak."
"Then, if you don't mind, I'll seek
The reason for myself, in Greece."
"Lady, if you will hold your peace,   924
I'll tell you what you want to know,
But I'd rather spare you such a blow.
Alas, you've made it all too plain
That, like it or not, I must explain."   928
Then, as before, the traitor sighed;
His tears flowed fast as he complied,
Craftily, with her request,
Knowing just what to say, how best   932
To make his falsehoods sound sincere.
"It grieves me very much, my dear,
To find myself obliged to bring
News that will cause you suffering.   936
Can't you guess how extremely bad
This news must be, if I'm so sad?
Believe me, I wish that I could keep
Silent about what makes me so weep   940
That nothing can hold back my tears.
I weep because the moment nears—
If I have the courage to speak out—
When you will no longer be in doubt.   944
Then you will know the reason why

I've been so unable to reply
To your questions. Now I'll put aside
My tender feelings." Then he sighed   948
Once more—but it wasn't from the heart—
And said what he'd planned to from the start:
"The messenger who brings bad news
Seems always to have no time to lose.   952
Your sister is dead. That is the fact."
"My sister's dead?" "That's what I lacked
The courage to tell you until now."
"Alas, poor girl!" "But you, somehow,   956
Must not give way to your heart's pain.
When sorrow comes we should not complain
Too much. Death will have its way.
All of us, good and bad, must pay   960
The debt we owe; early or late,
The time will come when we'll meet our fate—
We can't escape, so let's be resigned.
Death, in its season, came to find   964
Your sister; we should not forget
That she too had a mortal debt.
Grief and anguish must be borne,
For that is our lot. I pray you, mourn   968
Without excess what will come to all."
He thought to mix honey with the gall,
The bitterness that his false news
Had brought to Procne's heart. He used   972
Fine arguments to bring her relief
From suffering and soothe her grief.
But there was no way for him to reach
His wife with reasonable speech—   976
So far was she from being resigned,
She was very nearly out of her mind.
She said she was wretched, in despair,

Her sorrow was more than she could bear.　980
She struck her face, tore out her hair,
Cursed the gods, called Death unfair:
"Death," she said, "it was a mistake
To kill my sister. Nature will take　984
Revenge! You have desecrated
A loveliness that she created
Without equal. Death, you would do
Great kindness if you'd take me too.　988
Death, why are you so cruel to me?
Why won't you send my soul to be
With Philomena's? Only then
Will I know happiness again.　992
Death, why must I wait so long
To die? Surely it must be wrong
That I live on and never know
Anything but bitter woe.　996
If I should live a hundred years,
Never could I exhaust my tears.
Come, Death, and you yourself will be free;
You need only make an end of me.　1000
Are you too far to hear me plead?
Can you not help me in my need?
If you want peace, you'll understand
That you must do what I command.　1004
The rest of my days, remembering
This anguish, grief, and suffering,
I shall always dress in mourning black.
To do otherwise would show a lack　1008
Of deference to the custom here:
We grieve for those whom we hold dear."
Promptly whatever she required
Was prepared for her, and then, attired　1012
In black, she said she'd never wear

Different clothes, except ones less fair.
A sacrificial bull was brought
To please the gods; its blood was caught   1016
In a vessel—not a drop was spilled—
And when the animal had been killed,
She commanded that a fire be lit
In the temple for consuming it.   1020
Thus she followed in the ways
Of their ancestors in olden days,
Who made offerings when they adored
Pluto. That was the overlord   1024
Of the devils, and the ugliest,
Even more frightful than the rest.
Procne's command was soon obeyed:
At Pluto's altar a fire was laid,   1028
And in order to increase the smoke,
The custom of the Thracian folk
Was to give the bull then to the flame.
Procne vowed that the very same   1032
Sacrifice would be made each year
In hope that the mighty god would hear
Her prayers and treat her sister well,
Giving her peace and joy in hell,   1036
Where she would have an honored place.
As soon as there was but little trace
Of the sacrifice, its flesh and bone
Reduced to embers and ash alone,   1040
She poured the bull's blood on the spot
And put the remains in a white pot,
Each particle that could be found.
Then Procne buried it in the ground   1044
Under a marble coffin, dark gray,
Which then was lowered. When it lay
In place, an image dreadful to see—

A statue of the divinity—   1048
Was set up at one end of the grave;
For Pluto had the power to save
The wretched souls who burn in hell,*
And he rules the devils there as well.   1052
In letters easy to read and fair,
Inscribed on the marble was this prayer:
"Pluto, of hell the lord and king,
I pray you accept this offering.   1056
Have mercy, god, upon the one
For whom the sacrifice was done.
Wherever it is her body lies,
May her soul find favor in your eyes."   1060
So, with great devotion, Procne
Sacrificed to the deity,
Hoping by careful rites to save
Her dear sister's soul from a grave   1064
She wasn't in! She wasn't dead,
But the life Philomena led
Was a burden to her, bitter grief
Renewed each day without relief   1068
By that traitor, vile demon inflamed
By love. She was saddened, ashamed,*
Because he'd made of her his treasure,
Using his strength to take his pleasure   1072
From one he had cruelly betrayed.
She was very much in need of aid,
And longed to let her sister know
What had become of her, but no   1076
Plan for reaching her came to mind.
Even if Philomena could find
A messenger, deprived of speech,
How could she tell her woes and reach   1080
Her sister? If someone could be sent,

Procne would not know what was meant.
Philomena could not express
Her grief, and was under such duress   1084
That no matter by what means she tried,
She could find no way to go outside.
Why? What is standing in her way?
That peasant woman in the pay   1088
Of Tereus was there on guard,
And evading her was much too hard.
Always she was looking about;
Though Philomena tried to slip out   1092
A thousand times, she did not succeed.
But finally her urgent need
Reminded her of something not
Unimportant: she'd seen a lot   1096
Of spinning there, done by the two
Who guarded her, and so she knew
That for their needlework they possessed
Equipment enough to make the best   1100
Embroidered fabrics. She understood*
There was a means by which she could
Inform her sister of her fate.
Then Philomena didn't wait   1104
A moment, but hurried to the box
Where the old woman kept her stocks,
Her skeins and balls of embroidery thread.
Philomena went right ahead,   1108
Helped herself to everything there,
And then, taking the greatest care,
Began to work on her design.
The old woman gave no sign   1112
Of objecting to this activity,
And even was disposed to be
Helpful. She willingly acquired

Whatever she thought would be required   1116
For Philomena's enterprise,
Gave her the right tools and supplies
Of beautifully colored thread,
Indigo, yellow, green, and red.   1120
She certainly didn't understand
What Philomena really planned,
But admired and appreciated
The fabric that was being created.   1124
She herself worked on a bit
At one end, and saw the craft of it.
Philomena's workmanship
Depicted, first of all, the ship   1128
In which King Tereus crossed the sea
And came to Athens; then how he
Behaved there, how he took her to Thrace,
Brought her to a deserted place,   1132
Raped her, and after that cut out*
Her tongue. All this she told about*
In her needlework, and with great skill
Portrayed the house where she was still   1136
A captive, deep in the woods where none
Could find her. When her work was done
As perfectly as she could make it,
She needed someone who would take it   1140
To her sister. Philomena's grief
And anguish would have much relief
If she could find a messenger,
But no solution occurred to her.   1144
In that house they were only three.
The old woman would not agree
To go, or let her daughter be sent,
And Philomena never went   1148
Outside the house —she'd never found,

In six months' time, a way around
Their vigilance. But now so great
Was her desire to communicate,   1152
That the new signs she invented
Touched the old woman, who consented
To give whatever help was needed.
Large and small requests were heeded   1156
With one exception: even now,
She absolutely would not allow
Philomena to go outside.
By the king's order this was denied,   1160
And the woman had to keep her word.
But after long sorrow, hope stirred
In Philomena's heart; there would be
An end to her harsh captivity.   1164
One day, with her guard, she stood
At a window—now at last she could
Look out that way, or from a door.
That had never been allowed before,   1168
Since the tyrant, greatly to be blamed,
Had left her a captive, raped and maimed.
Not unhappily standing so,
Philomena saw the river flow,   1172
And between it and the woods, the town
Where her sister lived! Then tears ran down
Her cheeks and she was weeping so
Bitterly it seemed as though   1176
Nothing could ever comfort her.
If her guard could only discover
How to relieve Philomena's woe,
The woman would be quick to show   1180
Her change of heart. She felt such great
Pity for Philomena's state
That she had no wish to be unkind,

Except that, as always, she declined   1184
To let the captive go outside.
Many times Philomena tried
Other requests, and she perceived
That these were always well received.   1188
When it seemed a propitious moment,
She took her embroidery and went
To where the peasant woman waited.
Easily they communicated;   1192
Philomena's signs were understood
So well, it was almost as good
As talking in the usual way.
She touched the woman then to say   1196
In gestures her hope that she'd agree
To send the finished embroidery
To the city in her daughter's care,
A gift for the queen residing there.   1200
Her guard found all this very clear;
There seemed nothing for her to fear
In giving Philomena her way—
And why should there be any delay?   1204
She thought only good would come of it,
That Philomena would benefit,
As she herself no doubt expected:
Who, getting such a gift, neglected   1208
To give the donor a fair return?
The old woman was glad to learn
Why Philomena had done that work;
If help was needed, she wouldn't shirk.   1212
Philomena felt a great relief
From anger, bitterness, and grief.
She hoped that just as soon as Procne
Learned where she was, she'd be set free.   1216
Procne should have the news before long.

A proverb says that it is wrong
Not to be prompt in doing a deed
When one has a good chance to succeed;   1220
So had Philomena proceeded,
Once she realized what was needed
To start and finish her own task.
The old woman saw no need to ask   1224
Questions; it seemed quite innocent,
And her daughter could indeed be sent.
"There's something you must do for me,
My girl: take this embroidery   1228
And give it to the queen, right away.
Keep your wits about you. Don't delay
Going there or returning here."
Now Philomena's tears disappear;   1232
She takes great comfort from the thought
That when her embroidery is brought
To Procne, she will understand,
And deliverance will be at hand.   1236
The messenger really does her best,
Not stopping even once to rest
Until she reaches her destination
And nicely makes her presentation.   1240
When she unfolds the cloth, the queen
Knows very well what its pictures mean,
But she is not inclined to share
Her thoughts. Wanting no one else aware,   1244
She makes no outcry. The messenger
Is dismissed, and Procne follows her.
Not so close that she would be seen,
But not too far away, the queen   1248
Keeps a safe distance from her guide,
Until she finds herself outside
A bolted door. Quite out of her mind,

She doesn't speak or try to find 1252
Someone to help, but with all her might
Kicks it. Paralyzed with fright,
The peasant woman plays deaf and dumb,
But Philomena knows who has come. 1256
She gives a great cry and rushes past
The guard, who tries to hold her fast,
Shaking all over from fear as more
Blows and kicks weaken the door, 1260
Whose hinges yield with a sharp crack!
The woman cannot help but jump back;
She runs for fear of what is outside
And locks herself in a room to hide. 1264
Procne bursts in once the way is clear,
Shouting, half-crazed, so her sister will hear,
"Where are you, Philomena? I'm here,
Your sister! There is nothing to fear!" 1268
With tears flowing down her face,
Philomena runs toward her embrace,
And Procne runs with all her might
To meet her sister and hold her tight. 1272
"Philomena, come away with me!
Too long it's been since you were free.
Would you had never seen the day
When I was wed and taken away 1276
By that traitor who misused you so
That you cannot speak to me. Let's go
Quickly and leave this place of crime."
Then toward the city, all the time 1280
Lamenting, shedding tears, they flee,
Following secret ways where Procne
Knows that they will not be found.
Then, in a chamber under the ground, 1284
They grieve freely; no one else is there.

Procne says, "I cannot bear
To see you reduced to such a state
And have no way to retaliate.   1288
God grant that his cruelty to you
Receive the vengeance that is due,
That the traitor pay for what he's done!"
And as she said these words, her son   1292
Unluckily came into the room
Destined to be his place of doom.
He was a truly handsome boy,
But that day Procne did not enjoy   1296
The sight of him. In a quiet voice
She spoke words that were the Devil's choice:
"Ha! What I see here is a thing
That looks too much like that traitor king!   1300
Bitter, bitter your death will be
Because of your father's villainy.
You are the one who'll pay for his crime.
You'll have to die before your time,   1304
Unjustly die for just one reason:
Innocent though you are of treason,
And though you're not the one who's hated,
Never before has God created   1308
Anyone else, any other pair
So much alike—to that I swear;
That's why I will cut off your head."
The child heard nothing his mother said.   1312
He ran to greet her; when she was kissed
So joyfully, how could she persist
In the frightful plan she had in mind?
Nature ordains for humankind,   1316
As human law itself requires
And the pity in our hearts desires,
That no mother could have the will

To mutilate her child, or kill.   1320
But Procne's thoughts turned again
To that king forsworn, vilest of men,
By whom her sister had been defiled.
Far from reassuring the child,   1324
She said that he would soon be dead,
And with his flesh his father fed.
This was all that could compensate
For Philomena's tragic fate.   1328
Even as, lovingly, her son
Embraced her, the Devil's will was done.
Pride made her listen to what he said,
And do evil, cut off her child's head   1332
And give it to Philomena. They shared
In the cooking of the meat, prepared
Not in just one way, but in two:
Some they put in a pot for stew   1336
And some they roasted. When at last
The necessary time had passed,
The roast and stew were ready to eat,
But Procne was careful to complete   1340
All details of her preparation;
Then she offered her invitation
To the unsuspicious king. Her wish
Is that he dine on a special dish,   1344
She says; it's what he loves the best.
She would, if he doesn't mind, suggest
That for this occasion he'll require
Neither a companion nor a squire.   1348
Unless he objects to it, she'd prefer
That this once he dine alone with her.
She will take care of everything
Without any other help. The king   1352
Agrees, but he makes one request.

He says there must be another guest:
Itis, his son. Then, with Procne,
He'd need no other company.   1356
Procne replies, "I'll take good care,
I promise you, to have him there.
But you and Itis and I will be
Alone; the feast is only for three.   1360
No one else is even to know
Where we will be. And now let's go.
Everything's ready. I know the fare
Was prepared with very special care;   1364
It cannot fail to please your taste."
So, through her words, the king faced
The truth, but he could not have guessed
How he'd be treated as Procne's guest.   1368
Don't think she wanted to reveal
That his own son would be his meal!
Tereus does not hesitate
To follow his wife, who leads him straight   1372
Into the room where they will dine,
And her arrangements seem to him fine.
Procne gives him a comfortable seat.
She's set the table where he will eat;   1376
On it a lovely white cloth lies.
She brings him one of Itis's thighs.
Tereus carves and eats and drinks,
But he tells Procne that he thinks   1380
Itis really should be there.
"Where is he, lady? Didn't you swear
That he would come and join us here?"
"You'll have had enough of him, I fear,   1384
Before long. Itis isn't far,
And truly, my lord, your worries are
Quite useless. If he's not here yet,

He won't delay." Procne went to get   1388
Another piece of roasted meat,
And Tereus, cutting more to eat,
Continued, even as he dined,
Asking his wife to go and find   1392
Itis. "I am sorry to see
How you honor your word to me.
Clearly, you don't have the least
Intention that Itis share this feast.   1396
I have no messenger at hand,
And so, my lady, I command
That you yourself go seek him out."
Procne could not reply without   1400
Telling the king how he had dined;
Nor was she at all inclined
Now to fashion words to hide
The truth. "What you seek is inside   1404
Your own body, but not every bit.
There still remains a part of it
Outside you." Philomena, who'd been
Concealed in a nearby room, just then   1408
Comes out with Itis's head in her hands,
And doesn't pause until she stands
In front of Tereus. She throws
The head, from which the blood still flows,   1412
At his face. Knowing he'd been betrayed,
Tereus for a moment stayed
Silent and sat there paralyzed.
With shame and anguish he realized   1416
It was the head of Itis, his son.
He was ashamed of what he'd done.
His blood boiled and his rage doubled,
Bitterly his heart was troubled;   1420
He understood what was the meat

Procne had given him to eat.
The pain he felt at his disgrace
Made the color come and go in his face   1424
When he saw Philomena. But shame
Left him as quickly as it came;
The king's mind was entirely filled
With vengeful thoughts—his son had been killed,   1428
So Philomena and his wife
Would each pay for Itis with her life!
As the sisters savored his defeat,
Tereus, raging, leaped to his feet   1432
And kicked down the table; everything
Crashed to the ground, and then the king
Saw hanging on the wall a sword
And grabbed it. The sisters couldn't afford   1436
Another moment in that place!
They ran, and Tereus gave chase,
Threatening, as they tried in vain
To escape, that they would soon be slain.   1440
He chased them to an open door,
Where something never seen before—
A very great miracle indeed—
Happened, as the Fates decreed.   1444
Tereus was changed into a bird,
Old and scrawny, ugly, absurd.
The little claws that tried to grip
His sword were forced to let it slip.   1448
It was a hoopoe he became*
In punishment for his crime, the shame
Inflicted on a maiden—so
The story tells us. And we know   1452
That Procne was changed into a swallow.
Philomena does not forget her woe.
A nightingale, famed for her song,

She still accuses those who do wrong,   1456
The traitors, liars; seeks to destroy
Those who have no respect for joy,
And those vile felons who mistreat,
Slander, and abuse and cheat   1460
Honorable maidens, gentle, wise.
Woodlands still resound with her cries.
After the winter months have passed
And summer is beginning at last,   1464
Her sweetest song comes from her woes
And bitter hatred of her foes.
"Kill! Kill!" demands the nightingale;*
And here I'll end Philomena's tale.   1468

THE NIGHTINGALE

(*LAÜSTIC*)

Marie de France

The story I shall tell today
Was taken from a Breton *lai*
Called *Laüstic* in Brittany,
Which in proper French would be   4
Rossignol. They'd call the tale
In English lands *The Nightingale.*

There was near Saint Malo a town
Of some importance and renown.   8
Two barons, who could well afford
Houses suited to a lord,
Gave the city its good name
By their benevolence and fame.   12
Only one of them had married.
His wife was beautiful indeed,
And courteous as she was fair:
A lady who was well aware   16
Of all that custom and rank required.
The younger knight was much admired,
Being, among his peers, foremost
In valor, and a gracious host.   20
He never refused a tournament,
And what he owned he gladly spent.
He loved his neighbor's wife. She knew
That all she heard of him was true,   24

And so she was inclined to be
Persuaded when she heard his plea.
Soon she had yielded all her heart,
Because of his merit and, in part,   28
Because he lived not far away.
Fearful that others might betray
The love that they had come to share,
They always took the greatest care   32
Not to let anyone detect
Anything that might be suspect.
And it was easy enough to hide:
Their houses were almost side by side,   36
With nothing between the two at all
Except a single high stone wall.
The baron's wife had only to go
And stand beside her bedroom window   40
Whenever she wished to see her friend.
They would talk for hours on end
Across the wall; often they threw
Presents to one another too.   44
They were much happier than before
And would have asked for nothing more—
But lovers can't be satisfied
When love's true pleasure is denied.   48
The lady was watched too carefully
As soon as her friend was known to be
At home. But still they had the delight*
Of seeing each other day or night   52
And talking to their hearts' content.
The strictest guard could not prevent
The lady from looking out her window;
What she saw there, no one could know.   56
Nothing came to interfere

With their true love, until one year,
In the season when the summer grows
Green in all the woods and meadows,   60
When birds to show their pleasure cling
To flower tops and sweetly sing;
Then those who were in love before
Do, in love's service, even more.   64
The knight, in truth, was all intent
On love; the messages he sent
Across the wall had such replies
From his lady's lips and from her eyes,   68
He knew that she felt just the same.
Now she very often came
To her window, lighted by the moon,
Leaving her husband's side as soon   72
As she knew that he was fast asleep.
Wrapped in a cloak, she went to keep
Watch with her lover, sure that he
Would be waiting for her faithfully.   76
To see each other was, despite
Their endless longing, great delight.
She went so often and remained
So long, her husband soon complained,   80
Insisting that she must reply
To where she went at night and why.
"I'll tell you, my lord," the lady answered;
"Anyone who has ever heard   84
The nightingale singing will admit
No joy on earth compares with it.
That's why I've been standing there.
When the sweet music fills the air,   88
I'm so delighted, I must arise;
I can't sleep, or even close my eyes."

The baron only answered her
With a malicious, raging laughter.   92
He wrought a plan that could not fail
To overcome the nightingale.
The household servants all were set
To making traps of cord or net;   96
Then, throughout the orchard, these
Were fixed to hazel and chestnut trees,
And all the branches rimmed with glue
So that the bird could not slip through.   100
It was not long before they brought
The nightingale; it had been caught
Alive. The baron, well content,
Took the bird to his wife's apartment.   104
"Where are you, lady? Come talk to me!"
He cried. "I've something for you to see!
Look! Here is the bird whose song
Has kept you from your sleep so long.   108
Your nights will be more peaceful when
He can't awaken you again!"
She heard with sorrow and with dread
Everything her husband said,   112
Then asked him for the bird, and he
Killed it out of cruelty;
Vile as he was, for spite, he wrung
Its neck with his two hands and flung   116
The body at his wife. The red
Drops of blood ran down and spread
Over the bodice of her dress.
He left her alone with her distress.   120
Weeping, she held the bird and thought
With bitter rage of those who brought
The nightingale to death, betrayed

By all the hidden traps they laid.   124
"Alas!" she cried, "They have destroyed
The one great pleasure I enjoyed.
Now I can no longer go
To see my love outside my window   128
At night, the way I used to do!
One thing certainly is true:
He'll believe I no longer care.
I'll send the nightingale over there,   132
And a message that will make it clear
Why it is that I don't appear."
She found a piece of samite, gold-
Embroidered, large enough to fold   136
Around the body of the bird;
There was room for not another word.*
Then she called one in her service
Whom she could entrust with this,   140
And told him exactly what to say
When he brought it to the chevalier.
Her lover came to understand
Everything, just as she planned.   144
The servant carried the little bird;
And soon enough the knight had heard
All that he so grieved to know.
His courteous answer was not slow.   148
He ordered made a little case,
Not of iron or any base
Metal but of fine gold, embossed
With jewels—he did not count the cost.   152
The cover was not too long or wide.
He placed the nightingale inside
And had the casket sealed with care;
He carried it with him everywhere.   156

Stories like this can't be controlled,
And it was very promptly told.
Breton poets made of the tale
A *lai* they called *The Nightingale*.   160

THE TWO LOVERS

(LES DEUS AMANZ)

Marie de France

There came from Normandy an old
Story that was often told
Of how because two children tried
To win the right to love, they died.   4
A Breton *lai* preserves their fame;
The Two Lovers is its name.

As proof of the story, you can see
In the country we call Normandy   8
A mountain marvelously high
On top of which the children lie.
Close to the mountain, on one side,
There is a city, once the pride   12
Of Pître—so was named that land
By the king whose very wise command
Had built it. Honoring his will
The city is called Pître still,   16
And people even now are living
In the dominions of that king.
The valley of Pître that we know
Remains as it was so long ago.   20
The king had just one child, a daughter
Gentle and fair; he turned to her
For comfort when her mother died,
And kept her always at his side.   24
People did not approve of this;

The king's own household took it amiss.*
Hearing them openly complain
Caused him to suffer bitter pain.   28
With craft to meet his need he planned
How none should win his daughter's hand
Yet he himself be free from blame.
He ordered heralds to proclaim   32
Near and far to everyone
How the princess could be won.
The king would let his child be married,
But first, she had to be carried   36
Up the high mountain near the town
Before her suitor set her down.
As soon as they heard about the test,
Suitors hastened to request   40
A chance to win the promised bride.
Not one, no matter how he tried,
Could ever get beyond half way
Before exhaustion made him lay   44
His burden and his hopes to rest;
All were defeated in their quest.
The princess found herself a prize
To which no one dared lift his eyes.   48

In that country lived a youth,
The son of a count, and in all truth
Noble, courteous, and fair.
To become the best knight anywhere   52
Was what he wanted most to do.
Living much at court, he knew
And loved the princess. Eloquent,
He urged her many times to consent   56
To his desire, trying to earn

Her trust, have her love him in return.
She knew his valor, his gentle ways,
And that he had won her father's praise,   60
And so she said that she would be
His love, for which he thanked her humbly.
Often they would talk together,
Taking great care, although they were   64
So much in love, never to show
Their feelings, and let no one know.
But having to hide their love, they grieved.
The boy was prudent; he believed,   68
Whatever the cost, they must refuse
To venture all too soon and lose.
But very great was his distress.
One day it drove him to confess   72
How much he suffered to his friend,
Pleading with her to put an end
To their unhappiness and run
Away with him. That seemed the one   76
Way possible—he could no longer
Live in torment there with her.
But surely, if he asked for her hand
In marriage, the king's love would stand   80
Between them: he would not agree
To lose his daughter willingly,
Unless the suitor, to win his bride,
Carried her up the mountainside.   84
"I know too well," she said, "dear friend,
How that trial would have to end—
You are not strong enough to win.
But there is no good either in   88
Running away. I couldn't forgive
Myself if I should ever give

My father such good cause to grieve.
I love him too much; I couldn't leave   92
Knowing his rage and suffering.
I think there is only one thing
To do: I have an aunt I know
Could help, but you would have to go   96
To Salerno—she has lived there more*
Than thirty years. She's famous for
Her learning, and rich. For every kind
Of sickness she knows how to find   100
Medicine in roots and plants;
Surely this is our only chance.
If you agree, I'll write a letter
For you to take and give to her,   104
And you can tell our story too.
She will know how to counsel you
And give you some kind of medicine
To make you strong enough to win.   108
Then you can come back to this land
And ask my father for my hand.
He'll say that you are young and foolish,
And he'll consent to grant your wish   112
According to his own decree:
Only if you can carry me
All the way up to the top
Of the mountain, and you do not stop."   116
For the prudent counsel he heard
The boy gave joyful thanks, and answered
That he would, that very day,
With her consent, be on his way.   120

He went to his own home and hurried
To assemble all that he would need—

Money enough and fine clothing,
Packhorses, palfreys—summoning   124
Those of his men he trusted most
To travel with him to the coast.
Once in Salerno, he visited
The princess's aunt; when she had read   128
The letter from beginning to end,
She decided first to recommend
He stay with her a while. And so
She learned all that there was to know.   132
She gave him medicines to build
His strength, and by her arts distilled
A philter that would meet his need.
As soon as he drank it, however wearied   136
He might be, no matter how great
His burden, he'd not feel the weight
Because of the power that had flown
From his lips to his veins and bone.   140
She sent him back then to his trial;
He carried the philter in a phial.

When he reached his home, the boy,
Confident and full of joy,   144
Wasted no time at all, but went
To ask the king if he'd consent
To give him the princess for his bride;
He'd carry her up the mountainside.   148
The king had no reason to refuse;
He thought the boy would surely lose,
That it was madness to imagine
Someone of his age could win,   152
When men who were among the best
In valor had not passed the test.

The king then willingly proclaimed
The contest would be held, and named   156
A date. He summoned every friend,
Every vassal to attend
The ceremony. At his command
They gathered from throughout the land   160
To see the youth put to the trial
Of climbing up the mountain while
Holding in his arms the princess.
She, by eating less and less,   164
Prepared in the most useful way
She could. On the appointed day,
When no one had arrived as yet,
The boy was there. He didn't forget   168
To bring the potion with him. Then,
In a meadow not far from the Seine,
The king led his daughter through
The great crowd assembled to view   172
The trial. The young princess wore
Only a shift and nothing more.
Taking her in his arms, the youth,
Trusting her as he should, in truth,   176
Gave the maiden the little phial
Which she would carry for a while.
However sure the outcome seems,
I fear he'll go to such extremes   180
That the medicine will go to waste.
He reached the halfway point in haste,
Far too happy to remember
More than that he was close to her.   184
She felt his strength would not allow
Much more. "Please drink the philter now!"

She said, "My love, you cannot hide
Your weariness!" The boy replied,   188
"Dearest, my heart is very strong;
I will not stop to drink as long
As I can manage three steps more—
Nothing can change my mind before!   192
We would be seen by all the crowd,
And, if they should shout aloud,
I'd be distracted. They're too near;
I won't take time to drink right here."   196
Two thirds of the way up to the top
He stumbled and nearly let her drop.
Time and again the girl would plead,
"Here is the medicine you need!"   200
But trying, in pain, to reach the peak,
He didn't even hear her speak.
Exhausted, he went on until
He fell at the top, and then lay still;   204
His heart's strength had come to an end.
The maiden kneeled beside her friend.
He had only fainted, she thought,
And urgently, yet again, she sought   208
To help him, offering the philter.
But now he could not answer her.
Thus, as I have told, he died,
There upon the mountainside.   212
Crying aloud her grief, the girl
Picked up the phial again to hurl
The philter down. And it was worth
Much to that well-watered earth   216
And to the region all around,
For afterward the people found

Powerful herbs that flourished there.

The maiden, in her great despair,   220
Lay down beside her love, alone
With sorrow she had never known,
Now that he was lost forever.
So she held him close to her,   224
Tightly in her arms, and still
Kissing his eyes and mouth until
Her grief became a sword inside
Her heart. And so the maiden died   228
Who was so lovely and so wise.
Those waiting began to realize
That the two should long since have returned.
When they climbed the peak and learned   232
The truth, the king, in horror, fainted.
When he could speak, he mourned the dead,
And all the people shared his sorrow.
At last they let the children go;   236
Three days had passed. A marble coffin
Holding them both was buried in
The place that would forever tell
Their story. Then they said farewell.   240

Two Lovers is the name they gave
The mountain that was now a grave.
It all happened just this way
In truth and in a Breton *lai*.   244

HONEYSUCKLE

(CHEVREFOIL)

Marie de France

This *lai,* a favorite of mine,
Was named for the honeysuckle vine
And written to commemorate
The incident which I'll relate.   4
Many times I've had the chance
To hear or read the old romance
Of Tristan and the queen, who were
So true to love and to each other   8
And who, for their love, were sorely tried
Until, on a single day, they died.

Tristan, by King Mark's command,
Was exiled back to his own land   12
When, furious, the king had seen
The love he bore Iseut, the queen.
He stayed in South Wales for a year
And all that time did not appear   16
At court. But then, in his despair,
He couldn't bring himself to care
What might happen if he went back;
It was better to risk death than lack   20
The one thing that counted in his eyes.
This shouldn't cause anyone surprise—
A lover grieves and broods that way
If he is true and far away   24
From the lady who has won his heart,

And that's why Tristan had to start
For Cornwall. Whatever that could mean,
At least he was sure to see the queen.   28
He went through the forest, all alone,
So that his presence would not be known.
When evening came, it seemed all right
To seek some shelter for the night.   32
From poor peasants whom he met
He took what lodging he could get,
And asked if they knew anything
About the intentions of the king.   36
They told him that by King Mark's decree
The barons who owed him fealty
Had all been summoned forth to ride
To Tintagel, where at Whitsuntide*   40
The king intended to hold his court.
There would be feasting and good sport;
The queen was going to be there too.

Tristan was overjoyed. He knew   44
That for the journey she would make
There was just one road the queen could take.
As soon as the king was on his way,
Tristan went into the woods to stay   48
Close to the road where he could meet
The queen as she passed by with her suite.
Meanwhile, he cut down and squared
A hazel branch. When it was pared,   52
He signed it, using his knife to write,*
And placed the signal well in sight.
The queen would never fail to notice,
Alert for such a sign as this—   56
They had used it in another case

To indicate a meeting place—
And so the message would be clear;
She'd know her friend was somewhere near.   60
Earlier, he had sent a letter.
This is what he wrote to her:*
In the forest, where he had to hide,
He'd waited a long time to decide   64
How best to find her, where and when
They might see each other once again.
He could no longer live that way,
Cut off from the one he loved, for they   68
Were like the honeysuckle vine,
Which around a hazel tree will twine,
Holding the trunk as in a fist
And climbing until its tendrils twist   72
Around the top and hold it fast.
Together tree and vine will last.
But then, if anyone should pry
The vine away, they both will die.   76
"My love, we're like that vine and tree;
I'll die without you, you without me."

The queen, as she rode along the way,
Was waiting for something to betray   80
The presence of her friend, and spied
The hazel stick on a slope beside
The road. Understanding what it meant,
She called to those knights present   84
To be her escort, and expressed
A wish to stop a while and rest;
The traveling had made her tired.
The knights did as she desired,   88
And waited there while she withdrew

Alone, except for one she knew
Would keep her secret, the faithful maid
Brangene. After a while they strayed   92
Off the road and into the forest.
There was the one the queen loved best
In all the world, waiting for her.
Great was their joy at being together,   96
With time to talk again at leisure.
She told him that King Mark's displeasure
Had changed to grief at having exiled
Tristan; they'd soon be reconciled.   100
The king was sure he'd been deceived
By slander he should not have believed.
But when it was time for her to go,
Both of them wept in bitter sorrow.   104
Tristan went back to Wales and waited
Until he had been reinstated.

Because he wanted to express
The overwhelming happiness   108
Of being with his love once more,
What he had written to her before
And her words to him, not to forget,*
Tristan, a skilled harpist, set   112
To music. I will quickly say*
How people referred to this new *lai:*
Gotelef in English (which became
"Honeysuckle") translates the name   116
Chevrefoil. Here I've related
Just what the *lai* commemorated.

L A N V A L

Marie de France

I have heard another *lai*
Whose story I will tell the way
The Bretons did, to preserve the fame
Of a knight. Lanval was his name.   4

At that time the brave, courtly king
Arthur was in Kardoel to bring
Terror to his foes, the Scots
And Picts, who had been doing lots   8
Of damage to the realm; they crossed
Into England, and good land was lost.
In summertime he came to reside
In Kardoel, at Whitsuntide.*   12
Arthur gave generous rewards
To his courageous, noble lords—
Only the world's best knights were able
To have a place at the Round Table.   16
Wives and land the king supplied
To everyone who was on his side,
Except Lanval, and he had fought
Valiantly. Arthur gave no thought   20
To him, nor did his knights support
Lanval; the vassals of the court
Envied the chevalier, for he
Was generous, brave, and fair to see.   24
Some who showed him great affection

Would not have had the least objection
If anything occurred to bring
Him down. A very noble king   28
Was Lanval's father, but his land
Was far from where, at Arthur's command,
The knight now served. Lanval had spent
Everything he had, and was sent   32
Nothing from his lord. The knight
Would ask for nothing. Sad was his plight.
If Lanval's spirits were often low,
Don't be surprised, my lords; you know   36
That a stranger far from home, with no
Friends to help him, lives in sorrow.*

The knight I've been telling you about,
Who'd served King Arthur long without   40
Failing him in any way,
Took his war-horse out one day
Just for the pleasure of a ride.
Soon he found himself outside   44
The town. He dismounted near a brook
In an empty meadow. His horse shook
Strangely; Lanval undid the girth
And let him roll on the grass. No mirth   48
Did the knight feel, only his trouble.
He put his cloak, folded double,
Under his head and lay down awhile.
Nothing he saw gave him cause to smile;   52
He could only think of all he lacked.
Then there was something to attract
His attention: at the river's shore
Were two young women. Never before   56
Had he seen such beauty! They were dressed
In long tunics of the best

Dark-dyed silk drawn tight with laces,
And they had very lovely faces. 60
Two basins finely made of gold
The elder carried—you'll be told
The truth about this, I guarantee—*
The other a towel. He could see 64
How confidently they made their way
Until they were close to where he lay.
Knowing how to behave, the knight
Got up to meet them, to be polite. 68
But their greeting to him came before
He spoke, with the message that they bore:
"Sir Lanval, a maiden without peer
For beauty and wisdom, sent us here 72
To find you. This is her request:
Come with us now to be her guest!
We will guide you and take good care.
Look! Her pavilion's right over there!" 76
The chevalier agreed to go.
He'd leave his horse in the meadow
Where grass would keep it well content.
They led Lanval to a wondrous tent. 80
Never had there been one like this!
Not even Queen Semiramis,
When she was at the very height
Of her power, wisdom, wealth, and might, 84
Or the emperor Octavian
Could ever have afforded one
Of its panels. How much money was spent*
On the gold eagle above the tent 88
I don't know, nor how much would have bought
The stakes and cords that kept so taut
Its walls. There is not a king on earth
With as much wealth as the tent was worth. 92

Inside the tent a maiden lay.
A rose, when on a summer day
It first opens, or a lily,
Is not as beautiful as she.   96
The very sheets of her bed cost more
Than a great castle. The maiden wore
Only a shift laced on the side,
Fashioned so as not to hide   100
The fine, slender shape of her.
Partly draped in an ermine fur
Cloak, lined with a silk brocade
From Alexandria, she displayed   104
Her bosom, face, and side; they were
As white as is the hawthorn flower.

The moment Lanval came in sight,
The maiden called out to greet the knight,   108
And as he sat beside her bed,
"Lanval, my dearest love," she said,
"From my own land, which is very far,
I've come to find you. If you are   112
Honorable and strong in valor,
No count or king, no emperor
Has the good fortune, the joy I bring,
For I love you more than anything."   116
He saw how fair she was. Love's dart
Struck him, lit a spark in his heart,
Which was instantly alight. Then he
Answered her most courteously: 120
"Beautiful one, if it is true
That I am to have such joy of you,
If to grant me love is your desire,
I swear that whatever you require   124
I'll gladly do, if only it lies

In my power, be it folly or wise.
All your commands will I obey.
From everyone else I'll turn away.   128
There's just one desire in my heart:
That the two of us may never part."
When the maiden heard Lanval speak,
And knew that the one she came to seek   132
Returned her love, she gave him free
Possession of her, heart and body.
Now Lanval is on the right road!
In yet another way she showed   136
How much she loved him, for she willed
That his every wish should be fulfilled.
His poverty was at an end;
He could have all that he could spend.   140
Now Lanval's lodging suits him indeed!
All the wealth he could ever need
Would be his, and more. But in addition,
Lanval received her admonition: 144
"Dearest, be sure no one discovers—
I charge you this!—that we are lovers.
Should that happen, this is the cost:
Our joy will be forever lost.   148
You'll see me no more, will never hold
Your arms around me, if this is told."
Lanval said he would not be swayed
From keeping his word. She'd be obeyed.   152
On the bed beside her, the knight lay.
Now Lanval is lodged in a better way!
He was with her all the afternoon,
Until it would be evening soon,   156
But the knight felt very much inclined
To linger, if she wouldn't mind.
But alas, "My dearest love!" she said,

"It's time for you to get out of bed.   160
I will stay here, and you must go,
But there's something I would have you know:
Whenever you'd like to talk with me,
Just think of a place where it would be   164
Appropriate, not indiscreet,
For a knight and one he loves to meet.
I'll be with you as you request
And do whatever would please you best.   168
To no eyes but yours will I appear,
The words I say no one else will hear."
Happy because she told him this,
He rose to go, giving her a kiss.   172
The maidens who had brought him there
Had prepared fine clothes for him to wear,
And when he was newly clad, the youth,
Who was neither foolish nor uncouth,   176
Was so fair you could search many lands
And not find his peer. He washed his hands
With water they brought, nor did he lack
A towel. After that they came back,   180
Bringing food so he could share a meal
With his love. Lanval did not feel
The least desire to decline;
Everything was done with fine   184
Courtesy, all was to his taste,
And between courses, he was embraced
And given many kisses so sweet
They pleased him more than something to eat.   188

When they finished the last course,
They brought Lanval his well-groomed horse,
Saddled in a way that showed good care
Had been taken of it while he was there.   192

Lanval mounted, took his leave, set out
Toward the city again, but not without
Often looking back the way he'd come.
But soon the knight was overcome   196
With great fear; as he rode along
Thinking, his doubts were very strong,
And then Lanval began to feel
What had happened to him was not real.   200
When he came back to where he stayed,
He found his servants well arrayed.
That night good cheer was at his table;
No one knew how Lanval was able   204
To show such generosity.
Every knight in the whole city
Who needed lodging Lanval took care
To invite, and all were served good fare.   208
Splendid are the gifts that Lanval gives,
Lanval pays the ransom of captives,
Lanval offers minstrels fine clothing,
Bestows honors worthy of a king;   212
To every stranger and every friend
His noble kindness has no end.
And Lanval lives in joy and delight,
For in the daytime and at night   216
He can see his love whenever he wills,
And all his desires she fulfills.

Thus did Lanval's life go on,
Until, after the Feast of Saint John   220
That same year, as I understand,
Some thirty knights in a merry band
Were all out in an orchard, playing
Beneath the tower where the queen was staying.   224
Gawain was there to enjoy the fun,

And his cousin Yvain, second to none
In looks. Gawain, that noble man
Whom they all truly loved, began   228
To speak his mind: "My lords, we've wronged
Our friend Lanval—surely he belonged
With us today! Let's go invite
That courtly and most generous knight,   232
Whose father is a wealthy king."
They went to where Lanval was lodging
Straight away, and asked him please
To come and join their revelries.   236

Leaning against a deep-carved window,
The queen could see the orchard below.
By three ladies she was served
That day. Soon the queen observed,   240
Among the royal retinue,
A handsome knight, one whom she knew:
Lanval. She sent a lady-in-waiting
On an errand, telling her to bring   244
The loveliest maidens of the court,
And with the queen they'd join the sport.
Some thirty of them assembled there,
And they started down the tower's stair.   248
As soon as the ladies were in view,
The knights quickly came forth to do
Them honor, being very polite,
Welcomed them all with great delight.   252
And then the knights and ladies talked,
Joining their fingers as they walked.*
Lanval moves far away from the rest.
It has been too long since he caressed   256
His loved one, and he greatly misses
The touch of her and her sweet kisses.

For others' pleasures he does not care,
Wanting his own. The queen, aware   260
That Lanval is by himself, comes straight
To join him, and does not hesitate,
Sitting beside him, to make known
Her feelings: "Lanval, I have shown   264
That I honor you and hold you dear,
You have my affection; I am here
To grant you my love. All I seek
Is to know this makes you happy. Speak!   268
And my heart and I will be your own."
"Lady," the knight said, "leave me alone!
I don't intend to break my vow
To the king I've served a long time now   272
In good faith. I will not be untrue—
Not for your love and not for you!"
In response to that the angry queen
Gave an answer slanderous and mean: 276
"I see, Lanval, they must be right
Who claim that you take no delight
In women; I have heard it said
They please you not at all. Instead,   280
You have many a charming boy
To offer you what you enjoy.
My lord the king does wrong to trust
A coward whose unlawful lust   284
Discredits him; it's a great mistake.
His very soul may be at stake!"

When Lanval heard this, he was caught
Unawares, and spoke before he thought.   288
Bitterly he repented later
That in grief and rage he said to her:
"The ways that you refer to, lady,

Have nothing at all to do with me!   292
But it is true that I love someone
Who returns my love, and there is none
I've ever seen who could be her peer.
I want to make one thing very clear,   296
So that you'll really understand this:
Everyone who is in her service,
Down to the humblest maid, by far
Surpasses you, great queen that you are,   300
In beauty of body and of face,
In kindness, courtliness, and grace."
Furious at what she had heard,
The queen, without another word,   304
Back to her own room retreated,
Weeping. To have been so treated
Enraged and grieved her. She fell ill
And said she'd not leave her bed until   308
The king's justice had been obtained
Against the knight of whom she complained.

The king had been hunting in the wood;
He'd had a fine day, his mood was good,   312
But when he came inside the door
Of his wife's rooms, she fell on the floor
At his feet and vehemently cried
For justice. She claimed Lanval had tried   316
To win her to his heart's desire,
And being rejected, in his ire
Insulted her, boasted he had won
The love of such a peerless one,   320
So fine and proud that he'd consider
The least of the women serving her
To surpass the queen in quality.
The king was so enraged that he   324

On his most solemn oath then swore
That Lanval would appear before
The court, and if he couldn't deny
The accusation, he would die   328
Hanged or at the stake. The king
Rushed from the room, and summoning
Three of his barons, sent them for
Lanval, who had no need of more   332
Misfortune, as he mourned the cost
Of his betrayal: he had lost
The happiness that he had known.
He stayed in a room, all alone,   336
Calling and calling to his dear
Love, but she did not appear,
No matter how many times he tried;
It's a wonder he did not decide   340
To kill himself. She was pitiless.
Sometimes he lost all consciousness
But came sighing back to life again,
Weeping bitterly, and then   344
He would plead for mercy, cry aloud
In anguish, begging to be allowed
To hear her speak. When nothing reversed
His harsh punishment, Lanval cursed   348
Himself, cursed his mouth, which had spoken
Thoughtlessly; the promise broken
By no means would she forgive,
And then, alas, how could he live?   352

The barons whom the king had sent
Told Lanval what their presence meant:
The king commanded that he report
Without delay, to respond in court   356
To the queen's formal accusation.

The knight, in his desperation,
Reluctantly heeded what they said,
But wished that they would kill him instead.   360
When he appeared before the king
It was clear that he was suffering;
He did not speak. In a nasty tone
The king said, "Vassal, you have shown   364
Your treasonous disloyalty.
You attempted to dishonor me,
And you vilely put the queen to shame,
Slandering her with your boastful claim   368
That she has not the beauty of
Even the maid who serves your love."

Lanval protests his innocence:
He has committed no offense   372
Against the king. The knight affirms
That never, using the king's own terms,
Did he wrongfully approach the queen.
This, however, does not mean   376
He denies what he had boasted of,
But now, alas, he has lost his love.
So great is his sorrow, he desires
Only to do what the court requires.   380
The king was furious. He sent
For the other lords to give judgment,
When they'd considered this affair,
So none could say he had been unfair.   384
Among the barons, some were glad
To obey the king, and some were sad,
But their opinion was undivided;
They met, and all as one decided   388
There would have to be a formal trial.
But pledges would be needed while

Lanval awaited the chosen day;
They wanted to be sure he'd stay. 392
The barons felt it was wrong to hold
The trial with only the king's household
To judge the case. The king agreed
To convoke his vassals. He would need 396
Pledges, as he informed the knight.
Lanval could not provide them. His plight
Was desperate: he lacked support,
With no relatives or friends at court. 400
Gawain came forth and said he'd stand
In pledge to Lanval; his whole band
Of companions said they'd do the same.
The king told them, "I will claim 404
All of the land you hold from me,
Each one of you, as security."
They solemnly swore to have it so,
And after that they were free to go. 408
Those knights, who then accompanied
Lanval, thought it was sad indeed
To see him overcome by grief.
They reproached him harshly. Their belief 412
Was that love had led him far astray,
And they cursed it. They went every day
To see him: he might not be inclined
To eat or drink, could lose his mind. 416

When the court was ready to convene
In the presence of the king and queen
And all the vassals, those who'd stood
Security for Lanval made good 420
Their pledges. Many grieved for the knight;
A hundred would have thought it right
To free him: his case should not be tried.

But the king insisted they decide   424
If Lanval was guilty as accused,
Or were the arguments he used
In his defense ones they would allow.
It's all up to the barons now.   428
They go thoughtfully to deliberate,
Aware of Lanval's forlorn state,
Having come from a foreign land to fare
So badly, living among them there.   432
A number of lords approved of all
The king's complaints. The count of Cornwall
Said, "We agree about one thing:
It will make some weep and others sing,   436
But we are here to see justice done.
The king has accused a knight, the one
You call Lanval, of an offense,
And the knight protests his innocence.   440
When he boasted of his love, the queen
Took the knight's words of praise to mean
An insult to herself. Having brought
These charges, the king alone has sought   444
Our judgment. I will give you my
Opinion: we have no case to try
Legally, except for the fact
That Lanval may indeed have lacked   448
Respect for the honor that he owes
His lord. If by an oath he shows
His good faith, we won't be needed here.
The knight can have his love appear,   452
And then there won't be the slightest doubt
As to whether what he boasted about
Was really intended to demean
And insult the honor of the queen.*   456
If his words were true, the charge is denied.

But if Lanval cannot provide
His witness, I would have him told
He cannot serve in the king's household."   460
The judges then sent messengers, who
Explained to Lanval what he must do:
When his love appeared in court they'd know
If what he said of her was so.   464
The knight replied that could not be done;
Of help from her he expected none.
The messengers went back to report
That no witness would appear in court.   468
The judges had been told by the king
That they shouldn't keep the queen waiting.

When they were ready to decide
The verdict, they saw two maidens ride   472
Toward them, on horses trained to go
At an amble, smooth and very slow.
The maidens were comely, dressed in
Crimson silk over their bare skin.   476
The barons were not discontent
To watch. Gawain and three others went
To find Lanval; Gawain related
What had occurred, and much elated,   480
Escorted him to where he could see
The maidens—one of them must be
His love. But Lanval denied knowing
Who they were or where they were going.   484
The maidens continued on their way;
Without any hesitation they
Rode on, dismounting only at
The dais where King Arthur sat.   488
Their speech was courtly, and they were fair.
They said, "King, have your servants prepare

Suitable rooms, and you will need
To have their walls well tapestried.   492
My lady intends to be your guest
And must have a place where she can rest."
King Arthur willingly agreed
And called two knights, who accompanied   496
The maidens to an upper floor
To see the rooms. They asked nothing more.

Now the assembled judges face
The king's displeasure if the case   500
Is not concluded right away.
He says there's been too much delay,
And he's angry. But they answer, "Sire,
We'll soon have done all you require.   504
We had reached a verdict at last,
But the final judgment was not passed
Because of the ladies." Their debate*
When they reconvene is loud, irate;   508
They are worried, and quite afraid.

Two maidens, splendidly arrayed,
Their silk clothing freshly dyed,
Are coming down the street. They ride   512
Spanish mules. Then full of glee
Are the noble lords, who all agree
That this would be enough to save
Lanval, who's so worthy and so brave.   516
Yvain and his companions go
Immediately to let him know.
Once there, Yvain gives a happy shout:
"Good news for you, my friend! Come out!   520
Two maidens are arriving here,
And they're so beautiful, it's clear

Your beloved must be one of these!"
When Lanval sees them, he disagrees;   524
Neither one can he recognize.
He has not loved them; in his eyes
Their presence does not seem to count.
The maidens ride on, they don't dismount   528
Until they are in front of the king.
Their bodies, faces, and coloring
Are much praised; never was the queen
A match for the loveliness now seen.   532
Elegant, choosing her words with care,
The elder explains why they are there,
By saying, "King, we will require
Rooms where our lady can retire   536
When she comes to have a talk with you."
The king commands they be taken to
The maidens who were already there.
Of course their mules would receive good care.   540
The king took his leave and once again
Sent a message to his noblemen:
He must have their judgment. It was wrong
To let the trial go on so long.   544
Why weren't they able to decide?
The queen was most dissatisfied.

The moment of the verdict neared,
But in the city now appeared   548
A maiden such that never before
Had anyone on earth been more
Beautiful. A pure white steed
Carried her, and all agreed   552
That its elegance of neck and head
Showed that no horse was better bred.
It moved with a soft and supple stride,

And its fittings would have satisfied   556
The most difficult taste. A great lord,
Even a king could not afford
To buy the like, unless he sold
Or mortgaged the land that he controlled.   560
The lady wore a tunic over
A fine white shift. These fitted her *
So that the lacings on each side,
Carefully made to coincide,   564
Revealed her skin. Her hips were set low.
On a winter tree you see the snow
White as her neck and face; her eyes
Sparkled. Perfect in shape and size   568
Her nose and forehead, dark brows; her hair
Was curly and it was fair—so fair
That gold threads would not shine as bright
As it glistened, there in the sunlight.   572
Her cloak, wrapped around so she could ride,
Was made of dark silk, richly dyed.
On her fist a sparrowhawk; a slender
Greyhound followed close behind her.   576
Everyone in the city then,
From the children to the oldest men,
Came out to watch her passing by;
Having seen her beauty none would try   580
To joke about it in idle talk.
At a pace slower than a walk
She went her way. The judges saw,
With feelings of wonder and of awe,   584
How fair she was, their hearts alight
With joy. When she was out of sight,
Those who were Lanval's friends went straight
To find him, eager to relate   588
The marvel that they all had seen,

Whose coming, they were sure, would mean,
With God's help, he would win his case.
"She's not dark, with a swarthy face!   592
Of the women in the world, there's none
To equal the beauty of this one."
Lanval heard them; he raised his head,
Recognized the truth of what they said.   596
The blood rose into his face; he sighed.
His words came fast as he replied:
"That is the one I love. Now I
Don't care whether I live or die,   600
If she will no longer hold me dear,
For I am saved, when I see her here." *
And now the lady has gone inside *
The palace, continuing to ride   604
Until, as everyone watched, she stopped
Close to the king, dismounted, and dropped
Her cloak so they would see still better.
Courteously he rose to greet her;   608
His vassals did her honor too,
Coming to ask what they could do
To serve her. When they all had gazed
Enough and very highly praised   612
Her beauty, she spoke in such a way
They knew she had no desire to stay:
"A vassal of yours, King, I've held dear—
Lanval, the knight you see right here!   616
I don't want him to be denied
A rightful judgment. He's been tried
In your court for certain things he said.
The accused should be the queen instead;   620
I tell you, he never sought her love.
And as for what he was boasting of,
If they are convinced by what they see,

I trust your barons will set him free!"   624
The king replied that without fail
The judges' decision would prevail.
Every one of those lords admitted
That Lanval had to be acquitted,   628
Cleared of all charges, they report.
The maiden turned to leave the court.
People to serve her did not lack;
The king had no way to hold her back.   632
Outside the hall there was a place
With a marble mounting block in case
Of guests departing who might weigh
Too much to mount another way.   636
Lanval was standing there on top.
The maiden rode out and did not stop,
But Lanval, just as if he could fly,
Sprang up behind her as she went by.   640
And she, the Bretons say, rode on,
Taking the knight to Avalon,
That beautiful island. There with her,
Lanval, they tell us, stayed forever.   644
Since nothing more was ever heard
About him, this is my final word.

ELIDUC

Marie de France

I'll tell you all there is to know
About a story long ago
Told in ancient Brittany,
As it is understood by me.   4

Eliduc was a Breton knight,
The foremost in the land, by right
Of courage, courtesy, and valor.
He was also to be envied for   8
Having made a happy marriage
To a wife of distinguished parentage,
Noble and wise. For years they were
Loving and faithful to each other.   12
But circumstances led the knight
Into a foreign land to fight,
And that was how he came to care
For the daughter of the rulers there.*   16
The maiden was called Guilliadun;
In all that kingdom there was none
More lovely. His wife, who had to stay
At home, was Guildelüec. The *lai*   20
Now is called by everyone
Guildelüec and Guilliadun,
Although the name it had before
Was *Eliduc.* The story is more   24
About what happened to the ladies.

You shall hear then, if you please,
Everything that befell these three,
And why a *lai* records their story.   28

Eliduc was loved and honored
By the Breton king, his lord,
To whom he had sworn fealty
And served with perfect loyalty.   32
If the king had to leave his land,
Eliduc was in command,
Valiant enough to overwhelm
The enemies of his master's realm.   36
By the king's favor he acquired
Privilege; if he desired
To hunt for game in any forest,
No one could grumble or protest.   40
Often enough in such a case
A worthy man comes to disgrace
Because of envy. Whispered lies
Blackened him in his master's eyes,   44
And Eliduc was even refused
Knowledge of why he was accused.
Just because of that false report,
He found himself banished from the court,   48
And the chevalier could not persuade
The king he was unjustly swayed
By slander to forget the past
Of willing service. When at last   52
Nothing could make the king believe
His innocence, he had to leave.
Once at home the chevalier
Had his friends come without delay.   56
Then he told them how his lord
Was so enraged that he ignored

Eliduc's devoted service,
Surely worth much more than this! 60
Every chastised plowman knows
How the peasant saying goes:
"A fool on his lord's love relies."
A man will be both clever and wise 64
To give his master nothing above
Loyalty, his good neighbors, love.
Eliduc planned to leave the country,
Traveling across the sea 68
To England, where he was sure to find
A welcome. His wife would stay behind
And wait for him in his own lands.
All his household he commands 72
To serve her well, and he commends
Her safety also to his friends.
Once the decision had been made,
He would not change his mind, but stayed 76
Just to select fine clothes and gear.
Sad were his friends; they held him dear.
Ten knights were to accompany
Eliduc upon this journey. 80
When it was time for him to leave,
He said, in an effort to relieve
His wife's great sorrow, that wherever
He went he would be true to her. 84
With that they had to separate.
He took a road which led him straight
To the coast, and found a ship bound for
Devon, on the English shore. 88

In that region there were three or four
Rulers, always making war,

Among them a man of great power,
Who lived not far from Exeter.   92
This lord had now grown very old,
Without a son and heir to hold
His property. He had a daughter,
And had refused to marry her   96
To one of his peers, who then laid waste
The countryside in war and chased
The old man to a castle, where
He was at bay. No one would dare   100
Leave the protecting walls and go
To battle or joust with such a foe.
Eliduc, when he heard this news,
Felt no desire to refuse   104
The chance. They had come looking for
An opportunity of war,
And here was one so close at hand!
To the king in greater need he planned   108
To volunteer what help he could.
Afterward, when he'd made good
His offer, he could surely stay
As a soldier in that country's pay.   112
He sent a message to the king
And explained that he had come to bring
Help, if the king would have it so.
He'd left his country and wanted to know   116
Whether there would be interest
In his offer. If not, he'd request
Safe-conduct, so that he could proceed
To find another lord in need   120
Of his services. Greatly relieved
Was the king; the messengers received
A most cordial welcome. An escort
Was sent to bring Eliduc to court,   124

And the constable was told to give*
The knight and his men a place to live
Suitably. The king would send
As much money as they might spend   128
In a month. The king's men prepare
The escort, and soon the knight is there,
In the king's presence. Eliduc had
Welcome enough to make him glad   132
That he had chosen to come their way.
They had arranged for him to stay
At a house in town, where he had a most
Courteous and thoughtful host,   136
Who gave him his own room, all lined
With tapestries. Eliduc dined
In excellent style and took good care
That the poor knights who were living there   140
Should be his guests at dinner always.
His own companions, for forty days,
Had strict orders which would prevent
Their taking any kind of present.   144

Three days had not gone by before
They heard people crying out: once more
Their enemies were coming back
From all directions to attack!   148
There wouldn't be very long to wait!
They were almost at the city's gate.
As soon as Eliduc could hear
The sound of the people in their fear,   152
He and his companions armed in haste—
Not one moment did they waste!
Not counting Eliduc's own men,
Just fourteen mounted knights were then   156
Staying in the city; not a few

Were wounded, and there were captives too.
As soon as this small remaining force
Saw Eliduc armed and on his horse,   160
They were not inclined to hesitate
But armed and met him at the gate,
Saying, "My lord, we'll follow you
Wherever you go, whatever you do!"   164
"Thank you!" he answered. "Do you know
Of any road they'll use that's narrow?
We'll make an ambush. That would be best,
If there's a place you can suggest;   168
By waiting here we may begin
A battle we're not likely to win!
In any case, if we can choose
A better way, we've nothing to lose."   172
The king's men reply, "My lord, we could
Try the thicket near this wood.
There's a narrow cart road that they're bound
To take, once they have turned around   176
With booty to carry home again.
They'll pass close to the thicket then,
Disarmed and riding their palfreys
As they always do. Our enemies   180
Will thus be open to attack
At a moment when they can't strike back.
All we will have to do is wait
Until they come to meet their fate."   184
Eliduc said to them, "My friends,
Remember, if anyone intends
To win a battle or a war,
Or, for himself, great fame and honor,   188
He'll realize he can't refuse
To fight, even where he thinks he'll lose.
Each one of you has taken a vow

To serve the king, who needs you now. 192
Follow me, if you are true,
Wherever I go, whatever I do!
You can believe me when I say
No obstacle will block your way, 196
If I have to give my life to win!
If we can be successful in
Taking a portion of their prize,
It will bring us glory in men's eyes." 200
Convinced that Eliduc's plan was good,
They led the way into the wood
And prepared an ambush to attack
Their enemies when they came back. 204
The men in Eliduc's command
Were told exactly how he planned
To charge right before their foes went by,
And what would be their battle cry. 208
And soon the enemies were in sight!
Eliduc challenged them to fight
And called his companions to begin
The battle as if they meant to win! 212
Then they struck with power and speed,
Feeling, in their rage, no need
To be merciful. Their foes held out
Just briefly; they were put to rout, 216
Astonished at their own sad plight.
Despite their numbers, many a knight—
Their own constable included—
Was captured. They had not eluded 220
Eliduc's men, and yet these were
Only twenty-five in number.
With thirty of the enemy
Left to the squires, they were free 224
To take all the booty they desired,

And all the armor. They retired
Joyfully to the town. The king
Was up in a tower, worrying.   228
Now he was very much afraid
That all his knights had been betrayed
By Eliduc. He complained aloud
And, as he spoke, observed the crowd   232
Of knights approaching, every one
Weighed down by the prizes he had won.
Those who returned were many more
Than those who had gone to fight before,   236
So that the king could not decide
Who they were, and his doubts multiplied.
Therefore the gates by his command
Were closed, and men were told to stand   240
On the walls, prepared to meet their foes
With catapulted stones and arrows.
But there was no need of this. A squire
Rode up in haste and told the entire   244
Story—the role Eliduc played,
And the great valor he displayed—
Never had there been such a knight!
His men had taken in the fight   248
Twenty-nine captives and one more—
A constable—thirty was the score!
And there were also many wounded
Among their foes, and many dead.   252
The king heard everything about
Eliduc's triumph. All his doubt
Was turned to joy. He didn't stay,
But went to meet the chevalier   256
And thanked him for all that he had done.
Eliduc divided what they won,
Giving the captives to the king,

To his men the armor and everything 260
Except three horses that he chose
For himself, apportioning to those
On both sides who were in the fight
The booty that was his by right. 264

The deeds that I have told you of
Won Eliduc the king's great love,
And having agreed they all would stay
For a year, he promised to obey 268
In fealty the king's commands
And was made warden of his lands.

Eliduc was a handsome knight,
Valiant, generous, and polite. 272
The king's daughter heard his name
And all the reasons for his fame,
Which inspired in her such interest
She sent her chamberlain to request 276
The chevalier to visit her,
So they might come to know each other.
She found it hard to understand
That he had been living in the land 280
So long and yet had never tried
To meet her. Eliduc replied
That he would be happy to obey
Her invitation right away. 284
He chose a companion for the ride
And went to see the princess. Outside
Her room he sent the chamberlain
To tell her that he'd come, and then 288
He talked with the maiden face-to-face,
Most courteously and with a grace
That was proof of his nobility.

He thanked her for having wished to be   292
Acquainted with him, and even more
For sending the chamberlain who bore
The message that had brought him there.
Guilliadun, who was so fair,   296
Had taken him by the hand. They sat
On a comfortable bed to chat.
Carefully she looks, and cannot find
In her companion any kind   300
Of defect; his looks and manners seem
Worthy of the great esteem
She feels for him already in
Her heart where love's commands begin   304
To be emphatic and prevail.
Guilliadun sighed and she grew pale,
But not a single word betrayed
Her feelings; she was too much afraid   308
That Eliduc would think it wrong.
His visit with her was very long,
But then he took leave and went away.
She would much rather have had him stay.   312
Eliduc went back to his room,
Feeling, instead of pleasure, gloom
And anxious fear, remembering
The lovely daughter of the king   316
And how she'd looked at him and sighed.
Why had he been so long denied
Her company, so close at hand
Ever since fate brought him to that land?   320
Now she had summoned him at last!
At the same time he recalled the past:
How he had promised always to be
Faithful to his wife when she,   324

Knowing that he must leave her, grieved—
A promise they had both believed.

The maiden was thinking only of
How Eliduc must be her love.   328
Never had any man she knew
Pleased her so much—and she would do
Anything to have him stay.
Wide awake in bed she lay   332
All night, and did not sleep or close
Her eyes. In the morning she arose
And went to a window; she would call
Her chamberlain. She told him all   336
The secrets of her heart: "Alas!
By misfortune it has come to pass
That I love the chevalier whose name
Is Eliduc—the one who came   340
Not very long ago to fight.
I didn't sleep a wink last night,
But thought of him all the time. If he
Would only pledge himself to me   344
For love, with all my heart I swear
That I would have no other care
Than to do his will in everything,
And one day he would be the king   348
Of all this land. He is so wise
And courteous, if he replies
Coldly to my love, I know
That I will surely die of sorrow."   352
When the chamberlain had heard
What was troubling her, he offered
Loyal and very good advice.
"Lady," he said, "by this device   356

You'll know his mind: have someone bring
A ribbon of yours, or a belt or ring,
Perhaps, as a present to this knight.
If he receives it with delight,   360
He surely loves you. If you were
To love the greatest emperor
In the world, he would, I'm sure, rejoice
To learn that he was your heart's choice!"   364
But the maiden, after she had heard
The chamberlain's proposal, answered:
"I don't believe I could discover
Whether he wants to be my lover   368
Just by sending him a present!
What chevalier would not consent
To keep a gift, and readily,
No matter what love or hatred he   372
Felt for the donor? I'm afraid
That if I do this I'll be made
To look a fool. On the other hand,
From his manner we may understand   376
Something of his mind and heart—
How soon can you be ready to start?"
"Right now," he said. "Then you may bring
The knight my belt and this gold ring.   380
And greet him a thousand times for me!"
The chamberlain turned away, and she
Began at once to hesitate,
Thinking that she had better wait,   384
Then changed her mind; and so he went
Leaving the maiden to lament:
"Alas! My heart cannot withstand
This stranger from a distant land.   388
I don't know who his people are.
He could, at any time, be far

From here while I remain behind
To grieve. How could I make up my mind   392
So soon, in such a foolish way?
I met him only yesterday,
And now he'll receive my love with scorn.
And yet, if he is gently born,   396
Surely he will be glad to take
My present. There's so much at stake
For me in this, I know I'll lose
All joy in life, should he refuse."   400

While she lamented so and worried,
The chamberlain went with all speed
To Eliduc, and waiting only
Until they could speak privately,   404
Offered him the maiden's greeting
And her gifts, the belt and the ring.
Eliduc thanked the messenger.
He put the gold ring on his finger   408
And fastened the belt. But not a word
Was said. Eliduc offered
A return gift to the chamberlain,
But he did not accept it, and when   412
It seemed the knight would not request
Any answers of him, thought it best
To go back and see the princess, whom
He found still waiting in her room.   416
He told her the chevalier had sent
Greetings and thanked her for the present
"Go on!" she said. "Tell me, did he show
That he would love me? I must know!"   420
"I'll tell you everything I can,"
The chamberlain replied. "This man
Is certainly not frivolous,

But prudent, very courteous,   424
And will not easily betray
His feelings. When the chevalier
Received the gifts from you, he placed
The ring on his finger; at his waist   428
He fastened the belt, and with some care,
But said nothing to me. I didn't dare
Question him, since he had not spoken."
"He didn't take it as a token   432
Of love at all! If that is so,
I'm lost!" "My lady, I don't know,"
The chamberlain said. "But I could tell
That at least the knight must wish you well;   436
He didn't accept your gift by force!"
"You take me for a fool! Of course
I know he doesn't hate me—and why
Should he? The only wrong that I   440
Have ever done to him was just
To love him. And if for that he must
Hate me, he deserves to die!
Now there is nothing more that I   444
Would have you ask of him. What I'll do
Is speak to him myself—if he knew
How love torments me night and day . . . —
But perhaps he's soon to go away."   448
The chamberlain replied to this:
"The knight has made a solemn promise
And sworn that for a year at least
He would not ask to be released   452
From loyal service to the king.
There will be time for everything
To be said and done as you desire."
When she knew her father would require   456
The chevalier to serve him still,

Joy and hope began to fill
Her heart once more. She did not know
That Eliduc had lived in sorrow   460
Ever since he left her sight.
Nothing at all gave him delight
Except to think about the princess,
Though he remembered with distress   464
How he had promised his wife never
To love anyone except for her.
Eliduc's heart was racked with pain,
Because he wanted to remain   468
Loyal to his wife, and yet
For nothing on earth could he forget
Guilliadun. He could not doubt
He loved her, when he thought about   472
How beautiful she was, the joy
Of talking to her, nor destroy
His longing to hold her in his arms.
But if he didn't resist her charms,   476
He would be doubly in disgrace:
First, because nothing could erase
His duty to his wife; and he
Had promised the king his fealty.   480
So Eliduc remained in torment.
At last he called his men and went
To the castle for a talk, he said,
With the king. He really hoped instead   484
He might, by this means, see the princess.
The king was having a game of chess
After dinner, in her apartment.
He played with a foreign knight and meant   488
To have him teach his daughter the game.
He greeted Eliduc when he came,
Very well pleased to have his visit,

And asked the chevalier to sit   492
Beside him. He said to Guilliadun:
"You should get to know this knight! Not one
Among five hundred would be his peer.
I hope you will make him welcome here   496
And do him honor." The girl, delighted
To do her father's will, invited
Eliduc to come and talk with her,
Far from where the others were.   500
They were in love. But she didn't dare
Speak about it then and there,
While for his part the chevalier
Couldn't find anything to say   504
Except to thank her for the present—
No other gift had ever meant
So much to him. And then the princess,
Happy to hear the knight express   508
The fact that he had found it pleasing,
Said she had sent the belt and ring
Because of what she now confessed:
Eliduc already possessed   512
Her love and held her totally.
Even if he refused to be
Her lord, she said, she'd never allow
Anyone else to have her now.   516
So let him say what he would do!
"Lady, great joy is mine if you
Love me," he said; "to realize
I've found such favor in your eyes   520
Fills me with grateful pride. I'll always
Try to be worthy of your praise
And thank you for it. I'll be here
In the king's service for a year;   524
To him, in fealty, I swore

Not to leave until the war
Had ended. At that time I'd be free
To go home again across the sea,   528
As I would like to do; and so
I'll ask you then for leave to go."
"I give you thanks," the maiden replied,
"With all my heart. I'm satisfied   532
To wait, for surely you will say,
Before you have to go away,
What you intend to do with me.
Knowing your wisdom, your courtesy,   536
I love and honor you before
All else on earth." They said no more
That day, but both were well content.
The knight was joyful when he went,   540
Since he could come back to visit her.
Greatly did they love each other.
The war continued. Eliduc fought
With so much valor that he caught   544
The leader of the enemy,
And thus the king's whole land was free.
Eliduc's courage, his gracious ways,
And his good sense received much praise;   548
He was given, too, a just reward.

Three messengers came from his lord
Before the year was out. They told
The knight their master could not hold   552
The land except at dreadful cost—
His castles would very soon be lost
And all of Brittany laid waste,
If he could not get help in haste.   556
He had good reason to regret
Having, by evil counsel, let

Eliduc go away; he knew
That what he heard had not been true.   560
All the men who had betrayed
And slandered Eliduc had paid
Fully for their crime—they were
Exiled from the land forever.   564
Now the lord, in his great need,
Summoned the knight who had agreed,
When he paid homage for his land,
To bring what power he could command   568
To his lord's assistance in a war.
And never was such help needed more!

Eliduc received this news
As a heavy burden. He would lose   572
The maiden he loved so desperately,
As she loved him—they couldn't be
Dearer to each other than they were.
Yet nothing in the least improper   576
Had happened between them. Never wild
Or frivolous, they kept to mild
Pleasures of courtship, talked and sent
Gifts to each other, well content   580
To be together when they could.
But she believed and hoped he would
Be truly hers, for all her life,
Not knowing that he had a wife.   584
"Alas!" he lamented, "I was wrong
To come here. I have stayed too long!
If only I had never been
Near this country, or loved the maiden   588
Guilliadun, who gave me her heart!
Now, if we really have to part,
I'm sure that either she or I,

Or both of us, perhaps, will die.   592
And yet there's not the slightest doubt
That I must go, or live without
All honor, since the message came
From my lord who has the right to claim   596
My fealty. To disobey
His summons is also to betray
My wife. Now I must take good care
What I do! I might as well prepare   600
To go, since that's how it will end.
If I should marry my sweet friend,
I would offend all Christendom.
Whatever I do, no good will come.   604
God! It's so hard to go away!
No matter what anyone may say,
I'll never fail her. By her will
I'll go, or else remain here still.   608
The king, her father, can be sure
That the peace will hold his lands secure;
I'll tell him that my lord has need
Of help before the date we agreed   612
Would end my service in this land,
And ask him to yield to that demand.
After I've spoken to the king,
I'll tell his daughter everything   616
And try to do what she commands,
Leaving my future in her hands."
Having made up his mind, he pressed
The king to favor his request.   620
He asked for leave to go, and read
The letter in which his lord had said
That all his lands were under attack,
And summoned Eliduc to come back.   624
At this the king began to believe

That Eliduc really planned to leave.
He offered, in his great dismay,
A third of his lands, if he would stay,   628
And all his treasure. The king swore
To give all this and even more;
The knight would have good cause to praise
His bounty for the rest of his days.   632
"For now," said Eliduc, "I'll heed
My lord's command and serve his need.
He's called me from so far away,
I won't remain here to betray   636
His trust—I'll do as he desires.
If any trouble here requires
My services, I'll come again,
As soon as you ask, with all my men."   640
The king, most grateful to receive
That promise, said Eliduc might leave
And offered from his own household
Dogs and horses, silver and gold,   644
Fine silk clothes for the knight; and he
Chose among them moderately.
Eliduc, in a courteous way,
Said he would like to go and say   648
Goodbye to the princess, if he had
The king's permission. "I would be glad!"
He replied. A squire was sent before
The chevalier to open the door.   652
As soon as he came in, the princess
Greeted Eliduc no less
Than six thousand times in her delight,
And only then allowed the knight   656
To tell her what his visit meant.
He explained that his own lord had sent
A message requesting him to come—

Only thus could they save the kingdom.   660
Before he reached the end of the tale,
The maiden had turned deathly pale
And fainted. Eliduc, heartbroken,
Kissed her lips again and again,   664
Wildly lamenting in despair,
And wept to see her lying there.
He held her an endless time before
She could return to life once more.   668
"My dearest love," he said, "I pray
You'll listen to what I have to say.
You are both life and death to me—
All joy is in your company!   672
That is the reason only you
Can tell me what I ought to do.
Even though your father agreed
To let me serve my lord in his need,   676
Whatever comes of it, I'll abide
By anything that you decide."
"Then take me with you when you leave!
If I stay here alone to grieve,   680
There will be nothing in this land
I care about, and my own hand
Shall take my life!" With tenderness
In his voice, the knight tried to express   684
The love for her that filled his heart.
"I would be playing a traitor's part
If I should take you with me now.
In all good faith I made a vow   688
To give your father loyal service.
But when the year has passed, I promise,
If now you'll let me go away,
You yourself shall name the day   692
Of my return. If I'm alive,

Nothing shall stop me; I'll arrive
To carry out all of your commands.
My life is entirely in your hands."   696
Her love for him was very great.
She gave him leave and named a date
When he was to come back for her.
Tenderly then they kissed each other,   700
And exchanged their golden rings. Tears fell
As, mournfully, they said farewell.

Eliduc went across the sea,
With good winds favoring his journey.   704
His lord was overcome with delight
When once again he saw the knight,
And so were his friends and family
And everyone else, especially   708
His wife, who was so fair and wise.
But soon she began to realize
That something had happened, from the way
Her husband seemed never to be gay,   712
Never to welcome anything.
The chevalier was always thinking
Of the one to whom his heart was bound.
Never until the day he found   716
His love would he know joy in life.
He kept to himself and grieved his wife,
Who could only wonder and lament,
Not understanding what it meant.   720
Often she would ask him whether
Someone had spoken ill of her,
If he thought she had done something wrong
While he was away from home so long.   724
She was most willing to be tried

In public, if he'd be satisfied.
"Lady," he said, "I haven't heard
Anyone say a single word   728
Against you. But I must tell you this:
The king would let me leave his service
To come here only if I swore
I would return. And if the war   732
Had ended here, I wouldn't wait
A week, his need of me is so great.
There is hard work ahead for me
Before we've won and I am free   736
To go to him. Until that day
Nothing will take my cares away.
Never yet have I betrayed
Any promise that I made."   740
With that she had to be content.
Eliduc left his wife and went
To fight courageously beside
His lord, who by his counsel tried   744
Strategies which soon regained
The kingdom. When little time remained
Before the date the maiden had set,
Their enemies agreed to let   748
The knight make peace as he desired.
Then he prepared what he required
For travel. He would only choose
Three companions: two of them nephews   752
Dear to him, and the chamberlain
Who knew their secret, having been
Their messenger. That would do,
Apart from squires, for his retinue.   756
Each of them was obliged to swear
He'd hide all knowledge of this affair.

He didn't wait but started out,
Crossed the sea quickly and set about   760
Getting a message to the city
Where Guilliadun waited anxiously.
Eliduc knew it would be wise
Not to let anyone realize   764
He was there. He didn't show his face
But found a lodging in a place
Far from the port. Meanwhile he sent
The chamberlain ahead to present   768
His greetings to the maiden, and say
That he'd been faithful to the day.
That night after the sun went down,
Guilliadun was to leave the town   772
With the chamberlain who'd be her guide;
Eliduc would meet them both outside.
No one was apt to recognize
The chamberlain in his disguise.   776
He went on foot straight to the city,
Where the princess would surely be,
And inquired until he could assume
He would find the maiden in her room.   780
He greeted her and did not lose
A moment before he told the news.
As for the princess, when she learned
That Eliduc had at last returned,   784
Sorrow and gloom were cast aside.
Now it was for joy that she cried,
And many times kissed the messenger.
He said that he would leave with her   788
That very evening, and he stayed
All day until their plans were made.
They left the city when it had grown
Dark enough; the girl alone   792

And the young man; no one else was there,
And even though they took great care,
Still they might be seen, she thought.
Her dress was silk with finely wrought   796
Embroidery in threads of gold.
She wore a short cloak against the cold.

Shot from the city gates, the flight
Of an arrow would have found the knight   800
Where he was waiting, at the edge
Of a park protected by a hedge.
The chamberlain brought her to that place,
And to the chevalier's embrace.   804
Great was their joy at meeting again!
He put her on a horse and then
Mounted himself, and took her rein.
It wasn't safe for them to remain.   808
They left in haste, riding toward
Devon, where they went aboard
The waiting ship which carried no one
But Eliduc's men and Guilliadun.   812
Thanks to good winds and tranquil seas,
They made the entire crossing with ease.
But a storm arising just before
They were about to reach the shore   816
Drove them, by the terrible force
Of wind and waves, far off their course,
Their sails in shreds, until the mast
Bent and broke. They knew at last   820
That only heaven's grace could prevent
Swift ruin. They implored Saint Clement
And Saint Nicholas to see their need,
And Blessed Mary to intercede   824
With her Son, that He stretch forth His hand

And bring them safely back to land.
Yet they were driven by the will
Of the storm, back and forth, in peril,   828
Taking every moment for
The last. Then they heard a sailor
Shout above the storm, "My lord!
Because of the woman here on board,   832
Each one of us will lose his life!
You already have a lawful wife—
And this one too! You think you can
Break the command of God and man!   836
Yours is the sin, and we must pay.
I tell you, there is just one way
To save us all: the woman must be
Taken and thrown into the sea!"   840
Eliduc heard what he said;
Rage drove him nearly out of his head!
He shouted at him, "Son of a whore,
Filthy traitor, say no more!   844
Before you could take her, never fear,
I would have sold her very dear!"
The knight was trying as best he could
To do the seasick girl some good   848
By holding her close in his embrace,
But he was powerless to erase
The sailor's warning from her mind—
She would go home with him to find   852
A wife already in her place!
All trace of color left her face;
She fell unconscious to the ground
And did not stir. When Eliduc found   856
That nothing would bring her back again,
He thought that she was dead. And then,
Wild with grief, he was not slow

To seek revenge. He struck a blow   860
Strong enough to overwhelm
The sailor, who was at the helm,
And grabbed him by the feet to throw
His body to the waves below.   864
Then taking the tiller in his hand,
He held the ship to his command
And brought it safely to the harbor.
Even when they'd dropped the anchor   868
And lowered the gangway to the shore,
The maiden was lying as before.
To see her, anyone would have said
That she, beyond all doubt, was dead.   872
Eliduc, left to mourn and suffer,
Wished that he could have died with her.
He asked his companions to suggest
A place where she might be laid to rest.   876
He would not let the maiden go
Until he could have a priest bestow
Blessings on her, and see that they gave
Every honor to the grave   880
Where the daughter of a king would lie.
The men were unable to reply.
Seeing by their dismay that no one
Could help him decide what should be done,   884
He thought for a while, and said he knew
A place that possibly would do.
By dinnertime they could easily
Reach his dwelling, close to the sea.   888
Thirty leagues of woodlands hide
The place from view on every side.
The forest had a chapel in it,
Built by a very pious hermit   892
Who had come there forty years ago.

Eliduc often used to go
And talk with him. Now, if he buried
Guilliadun there, the knight would cede   896
A portion of the neighboring land,
On which a monastery would stand
Or else a convent. Every day
Those who lived in it would pray   900
That God be merciful and save
The maiden lying in that grave.
Eliduc sent for his horse, and when
They all were mounted, had the men   904
Swear on their honor not to reveal
The secret the chapel would conceal.
As they rode onward Guilliadun lay
In front of the grieving chevalier.   908

They did not stop at all, but rode
Straight along the forest road
And found what they were looking for.
They called, and knocked on the chapel door,   912
But there was no answer from inside,
However many times they tried.
Eliduc ordered one of his men
To make his way inside, and then   916
They knew why no one had replied.
The wise and holy man had died
A week before they came. It gave
The knight much grief to see his grave.   920
The others wanted to prepare
To bury the maiden then and there,
But this the knight would not permit,
Because, he said, "The saintly hermit   924
Is dead, and I will have to seek
The wise men of the land and speak

Of the abbey that shall glorify
This place. We'll let the maiden lie   928
Close to the altar, and commend
To God the soul of my sweet friend."
Hearing his words, the men obeyed.
Soon fine sheets were brought and laid   932
Carefully on the maiden's bed,
And then they left her there for dead.
Eliduc, when it was time to go,
Thought that he would die of sorrow.   936
Gently he kissed her eyes and face,
Saying, "My fair one, by God's grace
I shall lay down my sword and find
A way to leave this world behind.   940
A curse upon your life was I!
Beloved, you followed me to die!
My beautiful, you would have been queen,
Had you not taken love to mean   944
Total and perfect loyalty.
Now grief is all life holds for me.
I'll never leave you, my sweet friend!
I'll bury you as I intend,   948
And then, as a monk, return to pray
And weep beside your tomb each day."
So he promised her before
He left her, closing the chapel door.   952

Eliduc sent a messenger
To find his wife and say to her
That he was returning, but would be
Extremely tired from his journey.   956
The lady was overjoyed; she dressed
So that she would look her best
To welcome her lord when he arrived.

But from his greeting she derived   960
No happiness at all; he had
Little to say, and looked so sad.
She didn't dare to ask him why;
And so the first two days went by.   964
Each morning after mass was said,
Eliduc took the road that led
To the little chapel in the wood
Where the maiden lay as if she could   968
Just have fainted, yet had not stirred
In all that time or said a word.
It seemed miraculous to the knight
That her face remained so pink and white;   972
She was only a little more
Pale than she had been before.
But Eliduc could not control
His anguish. He would pray for her soul,   976
Weeping bitterly, and when
He finished his prayer, go home again.

The chevalier was unaware
That he had been discovered there   980
By someone whom his wife had sent
To find out where it was he went.
A squire had been promised, in return
For anything that he might learn,   984
Horses and arms as a reward.
So, after following his lord
Through the woods, he stood and waited near
The chapel, close enough to hear   988
Sounds of mourning from inside.
He didn't know why Eliduc cried.
Before his master had come out,
The squire went home to tell about   992

All he had learned: how Eliduc went
Into the chapel to lament,
And described the sounds of grief he heard.
Eliduc's wife was deeply stirred.   996
"We'll go to the hermitage today,"
She said. "My lord will be away;
I know that he intends to visit
The king at court. The saintly hermit   1000
Died not very long ago,
But surely my lord would not grieve so,
Although he loved him well, or make
Such lamentations for his sake."   1004

She said no more than that, and soon
Had learned the truth. That afternoon
Eliduc went to see the king,
And she set out at once, taking   1008
The squire along to be her guide.
Once at the chapel, she went inside
Alone; and there the maiden lay
Like a young rose. She drew away   1012
The covering and looked at her.
Graceful her body was, and slender,
Her arms and hands were smooth and white,
Her fingers delicate. At the sight,   1016
The lady couldn't fail to know
The reason for her husband's sorrow.
Calling the squire, she revealed
The wonder that had been concealed.   1020
"Do you see this woman's beauty,
So like a precious gem? It must be,
Surely, my husband's love for her
That gives him such good cause to suffer.   1024
Seeing such beauty lying there,

I'm not surprised at his despair;
My love and pity at the sight
Will take from my own life all delight   1028
Forever." Beside the maiden's bed,
The lady sat weeping for the dead.
She mourned, heartbroken at the loss
Of such loveliness. And then, across   1032
The body, a weasel ran from below
The altar. An angry squire's blow
Stopped it instantly; he felled
The creature with a stick he held,   1036
Casting its body to the ground.
Another weasel came and found
His dead companion lying there
And seemed to examine her with care,   1040
Prodding with his feet and circling
Close to her head. At last, when nothing
Was any use, he seemed to lament
Piteously, and then he went   1044
Out through the chapel door and raced
Into the forest. Soon he retraced
His steps to find his friend once more,
And now, between his teeth, he bore   1048
A bright red flower he placed inside
The mouth of the weasel who had died.*
This remedy in an instant broke
The hold of death. The weasel awoke.   1052
The lady had seen it all, and cried,
Before the animals could hide,
"Throw something! Don't let her get away!"
The squire was quick enough to obey,   1056
And with a blow, contrived to stop
The weasel; she let the flower drop.
The lady rose at once to take

The flower for the maiden's sake, 1060
And imitating what she had seen
The weasel do, she placed it between
The dead girl's lips, then stood aside
And waited. Soon the maiden sighed 1064
And opened her eyes. Her voice was strong
When she said, "I've been asleep so long!"
At that, rejoicing, Eliduc's wife
Thanked God for saving the maiden's life. 1068
Then she asked Guilliadun her name
And that of the land from which she came.
"I am from England," was her reply;
"My father is a king. But I 1072
Fell in love with a foreign knight
Named Eliduc, who was there to fight,
And when he left my father's service,
He took me with him—knowing that this 1076
Was a sin—and never told me about
His marriage. And when I found out
The truth, that he had a wife already,
It was such a terrible shock to me 1080
That I fainted. I still don't understand
Why he had me come to this strange land
To be abandoned and betrayed,
But a fool is easy to persuade." 1084
Gently the lady said, "My dear,
Nothing in all the world can cheer
The chevalier who grieves for you.
Believe me, what I say is true. 1088
He thinks that you are dead; his sorrow
Is greater than anyone can know.
I'm sure that all the time you lay
Unconscious, he was here each day. 1092
I am his wife, and his despair

Was mine before I came to share
The reason for it. My concern
Drove me finally to learn   1096
What it was all about. Since I've
Found that you are still alive,
Joy has brought my grief to an end.
Come with me now; I intend   1100
To give you back to your love once more,
And see him free and happy before
I take the veil. And so she led
The maiden home, much comforted.   1104

The lady told her squire to make
What speed he could to overtake
The knight, who'd gone to see the king.
Soon, after courteously greeting   1108
His lord, he told him all the news.
Eliduc mounted; he didn't lose
A moment to wait for company,
And was home that night. When he could see   1112
That Guilliadun had come back to life,
He gave most heartfelt thanks to his wife.
In all his life he had not known
Such joy as on that day alone.   1116
He and the maiden had good cause
For the happiness that made them pause
So often to exchange a kiss.
Eliduc's wife, seeing all this,   1120
Said that if the knight would give
Permission, she would retire to live
In holy service as a nun.
Eliduc could marry the one   1124
He loved so much. Her own desire
Was to have the land it would require

To build a convent. They all knew,
She said, that it really wouldn't do   1128
To have two wives—a married state
The law should never tolerate.
Eliduc granted her request;
He would do whatever she thought best.   1132
Most willingly he gave the land
To build the convent as she planned.
Not far from the castle, in the wood
Where the saintly hermit's chapel stood,   1136
Was the location that they chose;
There the church and other buildings rose.
The knight donated in full measure
Land and a large amount of treasure.   1140
As soon as everything had been done,
Eliduc's wife became a nun,
Establishing a holy order,
With thirty nuns who followed her.   1144

So Eliduc could marry the one
He loved, his beautiful Guilliadun.
After their wedding, consecrated
Fittingly and celebrated   1148
With a feast, they lived for many days
In perfect love. The two were always
Giving alms, doing good deeds until
All they cared for was to do God's will.   1152
He built a church on the other side
Of the castle, giving, to provide
Everything this would require,
Most of his land with his entire   1156
Treasury of silver and gold.
There the knight established a household
Of monks and serving laity

Distinguished for their piety.   1160
When all arrangements had been made,
Eliduc no longer delayed.
He joined the order there, intent
On serving God omnipotent.   1164
He placed his beloved Guilliadun
In his first wife's care, to be a nun,
And she was welcomed as a sister
By Guildelüec, who honored her   1168
And explained the Rule she must obey,
Telling her to serve God and pray.
Together they would always commend
To God's great mercy their dear friend.   1172
The knight prayed for them in return,
And often sent messengers to learn
How things were going on their side
And if everyone was satisfied.   1176
They tried in every way they could
To worship God as Christians should.
So living, they were not denied
God's grace and blessing when they died.   1180

From all that happened to these three,
The poets of ancient Brittany
Composed a *lai* to be told and heard,
So that its truth would be remembered.   1184

THE REFLECTION

(LE LAI DE L'OMBRE)

Jean Renart

I do not intend to quit
Poetry, and whet my wit
On idleness and dull repose.
Nor do I resemble those   4
Bunglers who can only write
To ruin; I would bring to light
Something in word and deed worthwhile,
And crass is he whose mocking smile   8
Salutes me when I use my skill
To rhyme a tale in which you will
Detect no vulgar insolence.
No one but a fool consents   12
To trade his talent for a joke;
And if, behind my back they poke
Fun at me, well, that's all they know.
Never can this finger grow   16
Long enough to equal this one,
Any more than from a felon
You can produce a worthy man.
But luck is more important than   20
Noble lineage for birthright.
Guillaume who tore apart the kite*
And burned the pieces down to bone,
If you recall the tale, has shown   24
That what I say is true indeed;
Many a man has greater need

For luck than for money or a friend.
Friends die; and one quickly sees the end   28
Of carelessly protected treasure,
While he whose spending knows no measure
Soon will see his wealth disperse:
When he wakes up at last to curse   32
His folly, everything is lost.
Afterwards he counts the cost
And learns to practice moderation,
So that, with luck, his reputation   36
May be restored without delay.
Therefore I'll compose this *lai*
For Miles, the Bishop-elect, whose will*
Commands it—to display my skill   40
In a worthy poem, and do him honor.
There's nothing that could please me more
Than to be challenged to employ
My wit on something I enjoy   44
As much as rhyming a romance.
They say good navigation lands
Good rhymes; once in harbor, why resort
To quarreling with the waves—that's sport   48
For fools. But those who reach the port*   (48a)
Of poetry are sure to win
The praise of princes. I'll begin
What you are now to hear if they
Leave me alone to write my *lai*.   52

Once there was a chevalier
Who came from the Empire—let us say
Between Lorraine and Germany.
I am sure you wouldn't see   56
His equal if you were to search
From Châlons as far as Perche;

Men of his quality are rare,
And one could very well compare   60
This knight with Gawain. He could claim
To have, no doubt, as great a name—
But what it was I've never known.
This chevalier could call his own   64
Valor and knightly courtesy.
He seemed, for generosity,
As if he'd wealth enough to burn.
Not boastful nor yet taciturn,   68
Despite his fame throughout the land,
He was not rich but could command
Enough to live agreeably,
And he placed riches with a free   72
Hand where there were none before.
Solely on the strength of rumor
Maidens and ladies prized him well;
Who could his advance repel,   76
Should he earnestly appeal?
Who'd discourage so ideal
A knight, so fine and debonair!
Whatever any social affair   80
Demanded, he did skillfully;
But quite another man was he
Than this, once on the battlefield—
His brave and wrathful strength would yield   84
To none. Once in his helm arrayed,
Well he knew how to parade
His challenge to a host of foes.
So far his warlike ardor goes,   88
This chevalier of whom I speak
Wished there were in every week
Twice the time for tournament!*
Never, by the Lord's consent,   92

Was knight so valorous as he.
Not like those who for poverty
In winter summer clothes must wear,
He gave more squirrel fur and vair*   96
Than many ten-times-richer men,
And every day he welcomed seven
Good companions, rarely less.
Whatever his household might possess   100
He was willing to give away.
He enjoyed—quite rightly, I say—
Falcon hunting when he could.
Rivaling Tristan, he was good   104
At fencing, chess, and what you will.
Long his desires did life fulfill,
And he was loved by one and all.
He was handsome, very tall,   108
Powerful and strong in grace,
But his admirers gave first place
To his valor—all a knight's should be.

She who of all has mastery,   112
Love, seeing the time was right,
Challenged him for the high delight
He'd had from ladies on his way,
Never taking care to pay   116
Tribute to Love when it was due,
Nor would he give her homage through
Humble service, and recognize
Himself a vassal in her eyes.   120
But now the moment had arrived:
She who will not be scorned contrived
To make him so feel her strength and might
That Tristan in his dreadful plight—   124
Even shorn to look insane—*

Suffered nothing like his pain,
Until she decided to relent.
Once the unerring bow was bent,   128
Straight to its goal the arrow came,
The beauty and the sweet name
Of a lady placed within his heart.
Now he must remain apart   132
From all others for her sake.
With many he was wont to make
Division of his heart, true lover
To none; then let him discover   136
He will henceforth wholly serve
The one he now thinks must deserve
For loveliness the ruby's place.
Her wit, her very noble grace,   140
The radiant beauty of her face
He can't, by any means, erase
From his thoughts by day or night.
Nothing now gives him delight   144
Save thinking of how fair she is.
So well had Love selected his
Conqueror, that just one sight
Of the lady had convinced the knight   148
There was not one on earth her peer,
And the memory he holds so dear
Still offers conclusive evidence.*
"I've been aloof," the knight laments,   152
"I've kept so carefully my reserve!
God would by this vengeance serve
Those who loved me without return.
To my sorrow did I spurn   156
Men vanquished by Love's mastery;
Now that Love has conquered me,
Whom she is determined to instruct,

No churl whose tooth was being plucked   160
By a barber ever felt such pain!"*
All he wants to do is remain
Alone to tell his woes and groan;
No one on earth has ever known   164
The torment that for Love he suffers.
"Alas!" he cries, "if I am hers,
What if she will not be mine?
If she should hear me and decline,   168
I couldn't live another day.
Whether I travel or I stay
At home, no pleasure dulls my pain.
Perhaps I would do well to gain   172
Favor with those who visit her;
By this means has many a lover
Come to joy from his despair.
Had she only placed a snare   176
Around my neck, her slender arms!
All night I dream about her charms,
As if she were embracing me.
But morning to reality   180
Wakes me from my great delight;
I reach out as if I might
Still touch her form that like a flame
Burns my body—but to claim   184
A treasure, it must first be found,
Alas; many have run aground
Like me on this. There's just one way;
I'll go or send someone to pray   188
Her mercy—my very life's at stake—
And beg her, before I die, to take
Pity on my cruel torments
And, by her benevolence,   192
Be savior of my life and mind.

If she should let me die, she'd find
Her court to be the less by one;
Surely from her heart must come   196
Pity, and sweetness from her eyes.
It seems to me it would be wise,
After all, that I go and tell
Her myself—to have a thing done well . . .   200
And who else would go so willingly?
We are always told necessity
And poverty can teach us best.
On these proverbs I will rest   204
My case. There's nothing to be done
But tell her myself that in her prison
My heart a willing captive lies;
And, before it wins love's prize,   208
Seeks no escape from harsh duress.
Then she'll have pity, and kindliness
Should lead her to be merciful."

He is now prepared for travel.   212
Two of his companions he picks
To go; their servants number six.
More than this I need not say;
He rides, wrapped in his thoughts, and gay,   216
Dreams of his purpose and his way,
Leads his companions all astray
From his thoughts and his intent—
They must not know what he meant   220
By this unexpected journey.
And so he rides on rapidly,
Hiding his thoughts and his desire,
Until they see a distant spire,   224
The castle that is her domain.
The followers hear the knight exclaim,

"Look how well that castle's placed!"
Not because he chooses to waste   228
His words on its thick walls or moat;
He says this only in the hope
They may be tempted so to praise,
For his delight, the gracious ways   232
Of the lady he has come to see.
And they reply, "How unworthy
Of you! It's an evil day indeed,
When a castle can precede   236
In praise a lady second to none!
You can be sure you'll find not one
In all the kingdom half so fair."
"Watch out!" they say, "were she aware   240
That you had so insulted her,
Better if you fell prisoner
To pagan Turks and went to Cairo!"
Then the knight, smiling, answers, "Oh!   244
My lords, not so fast! I needn't be
Treated with such severity;
This is no crime! I promise you
There's nothing on earth I wouldn't do   248
To have this castle, just this one
Alone. In Saladin's darkest prison
I'd gladly spend five or six years,
Could it be mine as it appears   252
Now—my own to keep, with all
That's hidden there behind the wall."
They say, "You'd be fortunate indeed!"
They didn't know enough to heed   256
The double meaning in his words.
The knight was happy when he heard
His friends reply so suitably.
He asked if they would go to see   260

The chatelaine. "It's only right,"
They answer. "Do you think a knight
Should let so beautiful a lady
Cross his path while carelessly   264
He turns away?" "It's up to you,"
He says. "I am quite willing to
Go or not. You set the course!"
With that, each of them turns his horse   268
Toward the castle, and on their way
They shout, "Aux dames, chevaliers!"*
A war cry fit for their intent!

So, at a gallop, off they went,   272
And soon were at the fortress. They found
A new courtyard, ringed around
By moats and a palisade—the best
Defensive walls. Across his chest   276
The knight had pulled his cloak aside
To show his fine silk tunic, dyed
Scarlet, rich with squirrel fur
And ermine. All three wore similar   280
Attire: white pleated shirts, blue flowers
In the garlands on their heads, their spurs
Glittering with gold inlay.
In summer, I think, there's no way   284
For anyone to be better dressed.
They did not stop at all but pressed
On till they reached the outer stairs.
Their servants, trained in these affairs,   288
Jumped down and went at once to hold
Their stirrups. Before he could be told,
The seneschal saw them in the court
And hurried from his lodge to report   292
The news to the fair chatelaine;

The knight who had arrived just then
Bore a name well known to her.
She blushed, but it was not in anger;   296
She was only surprised. Her maids
Had just arranged her hair in braids.
Instantly, from the crimson pillows
Where she was sitting, she arose,   300
Beautiful in all her grace.
Then her servants set in place
Over her shoulders a samite cloak;
Her beauty, of which so many spoke,   304
Was Nature's great gift. Even before
She'd gone as far as her chamber's door,
Her guests, who were in too much haste
To let the least time go to waste,   308
Had already come to find her there.
Her welcome made them well aware
That she was glad to have their visit,
And they were the more convinced of it   312
Because she had been on her way
To greet them. The lady wore that day
A white tunic; more than six feet
Its train extended, as her feet   316
Trod the fine rushes on the floor.
"You are welcome here, my lord,"
She says, "and your companions too."
I hope she has no cause to rue   320
This day, and may her joy be long!
The knight's companions were not wrong:
This was no lady to pass by!
They marvel, all of them, and sigh,   324
So beautiful is the one they greet.
Now she leads the knight to a seat,
Laughing as she takes his hand;

He has part of what he'd planned,   328
When he is seated next to her.
His friends, knowing what is proper,
Withdraw, at their own request,
To sit along a copper-bound chest   332
With two of her companions and chat,
Inquiring about this and that.
Meanwhile the noble knight, of their
Cooperation unaware,   336
Is thinking of his own affair;
For the courteous, debonair
Lady in such a skillful way
Answers whatever he may say   340
That he can well believe her wise.
Time and again he turns his eyes
Toward the beauty of her face,
Finding nothing to disgrace   344
His first impression. The evidence
Rewards his heart for confidence;
He sees her close at hand, and this
Confirms his memory's fair promise,   348
So truly beautiful is she.

"Dearest, most sweet and lovely lady,"
He says, "for whom by Love's command
I have put aside and banned   352
All others from my thoughts, what drew
Me here was this: to offer you
In faithful homage whatever power,
Whatever strength is mine—so prosper   356
My joy! There is nothing I love
As much as you—by God above
I swear it, may He save my soul!
You, and you alone, control   360

My fate; with all my heart I pray
That graciousness and pity may
Incline your favor to my need.
For piety may also lead   364
Those who pray to intercede
For those who only serve the creed
Of Love in perfect loyalty!"
"On my soul! My lord," says she,   368
"What does this mean? I don't know
How you come to be speaking so!"
He answers, "Lady, all you heard
Is true indeed; your slightest word   372
Commands me always—in your power
Am I." When he promised her
His fealty and love, a rush
Of color filled her cheeks. The blush   376
Didn't mean her wit could be despised:
"My lord, I would be most surprised
If it could in fact be true
That any man who looked like you   380
Was pining for love. No one could
Believe this! And if they should,
Handsome as you are, your fame
Would suffer for it! More shame   384
To you if your dissembling tries,
By throwing dust into my eyes,*
To make what's false pass undetected."
Fairly have her words deflected   388
His charge, caused all his hopes to fail—
Or that, at least, is how the tale
Was told to me. She leads him now
On a tight rein; this he has to allow,   392
For no one on earth could please him more.
Whoever treated him so before

Would have known vengeance swift and sure!
Her hold on him is so secure   396
He doesn't even dare to be
Reproachful, but resumes his plea:
"My lady, don't leave me in despair!
I've made you very well aware   400
How much your love would mean to me.
Why do your harsh words disagree
With the welcome that I saw appear
In your lovely eyes when I came here—   404
They had more pleasant things to say!
And, believe me, their display
Of courtesy was only right,
For, since first they saw the light,   408
They've seen no one who would do
Homage in fealty to you,
As faithfully serve you, as would I.
Sweet lady, tell me you will try—   412
For a year and a half let me serve
As your own knight, and when I deserve
Better, grant me the name of friend!
In much less time than that you'll mend   416
My ways, make me so valorous
At arms, at home so courteous
That by your influence I may,
If God is willing, learn the way   420
To win a lover's sweet reward!"
"I see that idle dreams, my lord,
Please you well. I only meant,
By welcoming you thus, a pleasant   424
Courtesy and nothing more.
I'm sorry if you took it for
Something I did not intend.
Certainly I could not pretend   428

Or ever wish to be impolite;
But this is the way it happens quite
Often—when a noble lady
Welcomes a knight with courtesy,   432
Treating him as an honored guest,
He takes for granted all the rest,
All that he desires to do.
This is proved indeed by you—   436
That's just the attitude I met.*
You might, with better luck, have set
A pigeon snare outside my door!
Even if the trial you asked me for   440
Should be three years long, never again
Would you have the welcome you had then;
No matter what tributes you designed,
Never again would I be as kind   444
As I was a little while ago.
Men should be careful not to go
Boasting before the prize is theirs!"

So badly now the poor knight fares   448
He doesn't know what to do or say!
"Lady, at least there's no way
For me to be worse off than before.
The pity that I'm asking for   452
Must be somewhere in your heart; I know
That Love always, however slow,
Grants the true lover victory.
I have gone rudderless to sea   456
As Tristan did to live or die*
As Fate intends, though always I
Have been sole master of my will.
And now I've been tormented until   460
Either you must save me tonight

Or I shall never see the light
Of morning again, so grieved
Is my heart, which without my leave   464
Has given itself in trust to you."
Then, laughing a little, "That will do!"
She says. "Never have I heard
The like! Now, not another word,   468
Since I see that you are serious—
Truly, by Saint Nicholas,
I thought it was just a harmless joke."
"You wrong me. Even if you spoke   472
Not of yourself but of some poor
Abandoned peasant girl, be sure
I could never be accused of this!"

But nothing that the knight can promise   476
Or say has brought him any closer
At all to having joy of her.
It seems there is nothing to be done.
In his despair his face turns crimson,   480
His eyes overflow with his heart's tears,
So that the red and white appear
Mixed together on his cheeks.
The chatelaine no longer seeks   484
To disavow her own heart's counsel;
Secretly she knows quite well
The knight has often found his way
Into her thoughts before this day.   488
To weep with him would do her good.
In truth, she can't believe he should
Suffer so much unhappiness.
"My honor, sir, would be the less   492
If I should offer love's reward
To any but my noble lord,

Who serves me well and honors me."
"Ha! lady, fortunate is he!   496
With this he should be well content!
I promise, if you'd just consent
For love's sake to be generous,
No one would think the worse of us   500
Who likes to sing or read of love,
But you'd be honored far above
All others in your time; love me
And you will show such charity   504
As those who seek the Holy Land."
"My lord, you make me understand
That it is wrong for me to stay
And listen to you. There is no way   508
For you to make my heart concede
What you are asking; though you plead
Forever, it would be in vain."
"Ah, lady!" he cries, "then I am slain!   512
I beg you—deny what you have said!
Do me this courtesy instead:
Grant me at least a token, something
Of yours to keep, a belt or ring,   516
Or else accept the gift of one.
No service that ever knight has done
To please a lady, though I lose
My soul for it, will I refuse   520
To do for you—and this I swear.
Your face, so sweet it is, and fair,
Claims my perfect fealty;
Whatever strength there is in me   524
Is yours, and in your hands my fate."
She says, "I have no wish to rate
The honor if I'm denied the pleasure.*
Your valor has in no small measure   528

Been praised, and long before this day.
You would only be led astray
If I allowed this to continue
Though you hadn't won my heart. I'd do   532
Then a kindness that would be
The opposite of courtesy,
And rightly could be called unjust."
"Lady, to ease my pain, you must   536
Give me a different reply.
Remember, if you let me die
For lack of love, on your soul lies
The guilt; your lovely, candid eyes   540
Will bring me to a cruel grave.
Now you must murder me, or save—
Set my fate upon its course.
Most beautiful lady, you are the source   544
Of all things dear to me; take care!"

His speech was courteous and fair;
The lady silently considered
That not unwillingly she heard   548
His plea, and that she did feel pity.
She can suspect no falsity
Now in all his tears and sighs,
But these are caused by Love, who tries   552
Him so hard. She is in fact inclined
To think that she could never find
A friend so debonair should she
Refuse him; now she wonders only   556
Why he had never spoken before.
But then Reason comes to the fore,
Arguing, on the other side,
That she would do better still to hide   560
Her weakness—or regret it later.

While he worried, seeing her
Far away and deep in thought,
He was by Love's counsel taught—   564
Love, who time and again displays
The subtle cunning of her ways—
How a victory might be won.
And so, while the lovely one   568
Was still rapt in her pondering,
The chevalier took off his ring,
Slipped it gently onto her finger,
And, inspired not to linger,   572
Spoke abruptly; her surprise
Gave her no chance to realize
That he had given her the ring.
Sure that she had noticed nothing,   576
"Lady," he tells her, "I must leave.
Remember what I've said; believe
That you command my life and heart."

With that the chevalier departs;   580
His two companions quickly follow.
No one but the knight can know
Why he left in so much haste.
Sighing he was, as he retraced   584
His steps; he found his horse and mounted
Pensively. Says the one who counted
Most, if he's to know joy again,
"Has he really gone? What happened then?   588
This knight has certainly no peer
For courtesy! I thought a year
Would seem to him not a single day,
If he were but allowed to stay;   592
And now he has gone away, contented.
Ah! And what if I had relented,

Yielded to him in word or deed!
Since counterfeit can so mislead,   596
Take no one on earth as he appears!
If I had really, by those tears
And lying sighs, been taken in,
On my soul, I swear he'd win   600
His triumph when the price was low.
Could anyone in the world be so
Clever at lies and trickery?"
And at that very moment she   604
Looked at her hand, and saw the ring.
Every drop of blood went rushing
Down to her very toes! Never
Had anything astonished her   608
So much, or seemed to her so strange.
Her color in an instant changed
From crimson to a pallid white.
"God help me!" she says; "can I be right?"   612
Isn't this the ring he wore?
Unless my mind fails me, once before
I saw it—on his hand! I know
I did, a little while ago!   616
Why has he given it to me?
Because I never would agree,
He has assumed a lover's part.
He's a past master of this art;   620
I wonder where he went to school!
How did he do it? What a fool
I must have been, completely blind—
Otherwise he could never find   624
A way of giving mc his ring!
And now that he has done this thing,
He'll claim that he has won my love.
Is it really true? Am I his love?   628

No! He'd say so quite in vain.
I'll have him come back, and I'll explain—
Somehow he must be made to see—
I'll tell him I can never be   632
His friend, unless he takes it back.
In this, I'm sure, he won't lack
Courtesy, if he fears my anger."

She ordered a servant sent to her   636
Ready to ride—they must not waste
A moment. Very soon, in haste,
A squire appeared. She said, "Please go
After that knight. If you're not slow   640
I'm sure you can overtake him. Say
He must, if he cares for me, obey
My will, and instantly return.
There's something of very great concern   644
To him about which I would speak."
"My lady, I'll do my best to seek
The knight and carry out your orders."
So he gallops off and spurs   648
After the chevalier, in torment
For love of the very one who sent
The squire to find him. He was no more
Than a league away from her before   652
The messenger came to turn him back.
No one could say he showed a lack
Of willingness—he had good cause
To thank his stars. Nor did he pause   656
To ask any questions; he preferred
To believe that the ring offered
Only an excuse to summon
Him back, and that the true reason   660
Must certainly be her desire

To see him again. En route her squire
Became acquainted with the knight.
God! But the future now seemed bright—   664
Except for the tormenting thought
That she might, after all, have sought
To give him back his ring. He vows
To see himself, before he allows   668
That to happen, a monk at Cîteaux!*
"I can't believe she'll treat me so
Harshly for what I did." He rides
Onward, and soon his pleasure hides   672
The thought that troubled him before.
Now he has come back to the door
By which he'd left the lady's fortress.

The chatelaine, in great distress,   676
Fighting her own desires, now
Leaves her chamber and, walking down
The long stairs slowly, one by one,
Plans what should be said and done   680
To reprove the chevalier coming
Into the outer court; his ring
Still shines on her finger. "This knight
May possibly refuse, in spite   684
Of all I can say; I might not make
Him do my will. So I'd best not take
The bull by the horns. I'll see*
First that we talk in privacy   688
Beside the well. That way, if he
Shows me the least discourtesy,
I'll end the matter then and there.
But how? I won't solve this affair   692
Just by dropping it on the ground.
Where then? It never must be found.

In the well! Thus, as if it were
A passing dream, I won't suffer   696
From what could, perhaps, be said of me.
Haven't I lived honorably
For a long time now with my own lord?
If this one thinks that I'll reward   700
His show of gallantry, his sighs,
That he can carry off the prize
Of my love on one single visit—
He wouldn't have overworked his wit   704
To win, if that were proven true!"*

Just then the chevalier, who knew
Nothing about all this, appeared.
He dismounted, and as if he feared   708
Nothing, confident and gay,
Ran to greet her just the way
Knights with ladies have always done.
Neither his friends nor anyone   712
From the household comes to interfere.
"I greet the lady without peer,
To whom I belong, now and always!"
But she is not bowled over by praise,*   716
Nor willing to take him at his word;
Many things has the lady heard
Today that touched her, close to her heart.
"Sir," she says, leading him apart,   720
"Let us sit here beside the well
And talk." What evil ever befell
A man after so kind a greeting!
Now he is sure, thanks to his ring,   724
That he is on the way to success.
His confidence will grow much less
Before his hopes begin to prosper!

As he goes to sit down next to her,   728
He hears something which disagrees
With his delight: "My lord, if you please,
There is something I don't understand:
I have your ring, here in my hand;   732
Why have you given it to me?"
He says, "Sweet lady, it will be
There on your finger when I go.
I promise you, I want you to know—   736
You must believe that this is true—
The ring is magnified in value,
Having been yours. If you please,
This summer all my enemies   740
Will be, not to their joy, aware
That you have granted me your fair
Love, as mine belongs to you."
"In God's name, sir! That isn't true!"   744
She says, "You have it entirely wrong!
I'll never leave this house as long
As I live, if you should dare presume
To boast about my love to plume   748
Your pride! Not for anything on earth!
All that you have tried is worth
Nothing; you're very far off the track!
Here! I want you to take back   752
The ring you gave to me in vain.
Woe betide you if you claim
My love because I wore it once!"
Now he grieves who thought he had won;   756
He who had conquered all laments:
"My fame will do a harsh penance
If what I heard is really true.
Never did any joy I knew   760
So quickly turn to bitter pain."

"Surely, my lord, you can't complain
That any dishonor would be found
In you for this. We are not bound   764
By ties of love or lineage;
I will commit no sacrilege
If I return the ring to you.
And there is nothing you can do   768
But take it back. I can't allow
Your tribute if I disavow
Your love, as I am sure I must."
"God!" he says, "were I to thrust   772
A knife blade deep into my thigh,
It wouldn't inflict such pain as I
Feel from these words. It is no great
Triumph to annihilate   776
An enemy who is on the ground!
By my heart's passion I am bound
And made to suffer cruel torment;
Any woman must repent   780
Who tries to make me take it back.
No! Let God forever rack
My soul if I agree to this!
One thing I can surely promise   784
Is that when I've left here, on your hand
The ring will be, at your command
My heart—and in your service none
Will rival my heart and ring as one."   788
The lady says, "Now you abuse
My patience! Take care; or you will lose
Whatever friendship I may still
Offer you, if against my will   792
You make me angry by insisting.
I say you must take back the ring."

"Never!" "You will! Unless, of course,
Your arguments should turn to force,   796
And try to make my will defer
To yours, as if indeed you were
More than my master and my lord.
Here!" "What you ask I can't afford."   800
"Take it!" "Never will I agree."
"Then do you hope to conquer me
By force?" "No, lady, that's not true;
God help me, I've no power to do   804
Anything of the kind, alas!
But boorishness and grief would pass
Away forever, I am sure,
If you would give me hope to cure   808
My pain, not drive me to defeat."
"My lord," she answers, "you could beat
Your head on stone to more avail;
By no means can you prevail   812
On me, as you know very well."
"To please you I must learn to tell
Ingenious stories like Renart.*
Were I to hang, it would be far   816
Better than to accept the ring!
Why must we go on quarreling?
You know by now I won't agree."
"My words, as far as I can see,   820
Do nothing more than make you stubborn.
You won't allow me to return
The ring, no matter what I say.
Now by your promise to obey   824
My commands in everything,
I charge you to take back the ring,
And by the faith you owe to Love."

He does not miss the meaning of   828
Her words; either he yields to her
Or else she will no doubt consider
All his vows but empty lies.
"Oh, God!" he says, "which way lies   832
The lesser evil? If I leave
The ring with her, she won't believe
My love. It would be to no avail.
Lovers and pastry cooks both fail   836
When they press too hard what they embrace!*
Protest would only mean disgrace.
She claims the obedience I swore
And the ring cannot be placed before   840
Honor; I'll have to take it back.
Otherwise I'll appear to lack
The courtesy that I should show
The lady to whom by right I owe   844
This tribute of my love for her.
Even when it is on my finger,
It will be my lady's nonetheless.
I am indeed dishonored unless   848
I do whatever she may choose
To ask; no lover can refuse
Faithful obedience to his lady.
No one can say he serves Love truly   852
Who leaves what he can do undone.
So I must, for this same reason,
Yield to all that she commands
And place myself wholly in her hands,   856
Inclining my own will to hers."
He does not speak her name but defers*
To her wish: "Lady, I will take
The ring, if you will let me make   860

One condition: that I am free
To do with it what pleases me.
I will have joy remembering
You wore it once." She says, "The ring   864
Is yours, to give away or keep."
Don't think that rusty or asleep
Were the wits of that most valiant knight.
He had hope enough to feel delight   868
As he took the ring back thoughtfully
And said, looking at it sweetly,
"Lady, you have been very kind!
The gold has not turned black, I find,   872
Since it came from such a lovely hand!"
She smiled, believing that he planned
To put it on his finger again.
But he did something better, and then   876
Was granted joy, as I shall tell.
He leaned his elbow on the well,
Which was no more than nine feet deep,
And there below him he could see   880
In the water, glittering and clear,
The image of someone who was dear
To him above all else on earth.
He said, "This ring may be of worth   884
To someone; I won't take it away,
But my sweet lady here today
Shall have it, next to you the one
I love best." "But how could she have come?   888
I thought that we were quite alone!"
"Soon, I promise, you shall be shown
How courteous she is, and fair."
"But where, in God's name?" "Look down there!   892
Don't you see your reflection waiting?"

The chevalier held up the ring:
"It is for you to keep, sweet friend!
My lady refused me in the end,   896
But you will not disappoint me so."
As soon as the ring fell, the shadow
Vanished in the rippled waters.
Then the knight said, "It is hers.   900
By this means the ring restores
My pride, for something that is yours
Received it; and this does me honor.
I only wish there were a door   904
Down there in the well. She'd come here,
And I'd give the one I hold dear
The thanks from me that she deserves."

Now, by God, his courtesy serves   908
To lead the knight to happiness.
Nothing could ever more impress
Or give more pleasure to the lady.
Restored to joy, she ardently*   912
Lifts her eyes to meet his own.
Many times it has been shown
That courtesy wins a sweet reward.
"I have behaved so cruelly toward   916
This knight; now love begins to sway
My heart. For ever since the day
Of Adam's fall, no one has been
So gallant, nor will be again.   920
Who would have imagined such a thing?
Since he gave my reflection the ring
For love of me, I'm sure that I
Cannot and really shouldn't deny   924
His valor the gift of my true love.

And why delay? Worthy above
All others to have love's victory
Is the peerless knight whose gallantry   928
Conquered my heart with a little ring."
You may be sure he finds no sting
In her words when she says, "My sweet friend,
Not a moment more can I defend   932
My heart against your courtesy
And the way that you have honored me,
Sending your ring to my reflection.
Now, with all my heart's affection,   936
I'll give you one of mine. Take it so.
I think you'll like it as much, although
It cannot compare in worth to yours."
The knight says, "If they made me lord   940
Of the whole empire, less were my joy."

The two beside the well enjoy
Much of love's pleasure then and there.
From all the kisses that they share   944
They feel the sweetness in their hearts.
Their eyes do not fail to play their parts—
And that's the very least one can say!
In all those games that hands may play   948
Their mastery is now complete.
What they must save for when they meet
More privately will suit them well.

But JEHAN RENART is not to tell   952
Or even think further of these two.
If he has nothing else to do
Let him find another tale to write.
Since their desires and Love unite,   956

Surely there needn't be a text
For the sport that will be coming next.
All they have to do is try it—
And let the rest of us keep quiet!   960
Here I'll hand over this account
To raconteurs who know how to count.*

THE CHATELAINE OF VERGI

(LA CHASTELAINE DE VERGI)

Anonymous

There are people who pretend
Loyalty, say they intend
To keep your confidence so well
That you may without danger tell 4
Your secrets; and when they discover
Proof that someone has a lover
Make it their pleasure and their pride
To send the news out far and wide, 8
And afterward make fun of those
Who lose their joy because they chose
To have it known. The greater the love
The more will be the sorrow of 12
The true lover who must start
Doubting the one who rules his heart.
And oftentimes such harm is done
By this that love will quickly run 16
Its course, to end in grief and shame.
In just that way misfortune came
To a valiant knight in Burgundy
And to the lady of Vergi. 20

True was his love, and to his plea
Consenting, she said he must agree
To one condition: on the day
And hour that he would give away 24
Their secret, he would lose her pledge

Of love and that sweet privilege
Granted to his heart's desire.
So that they would not require   28
A messenger, the chevalier
On certain evenings was to stay
In a nearby orchard, nor withdraw
From its shelter until he saw   32
Coming toward his hiding place
Her little dog. In that case
The knight continued on his way
Into her room without delay,   36
Knowing that he need have no fear
That anyone would ever appear,*
Except the chatelaine alone.
For a long time they called their own   40
Love's happiness, and never let
Anyone surprise their secret.

Because the chevalier was handsome
And valorous, he had become   44
Known to the duke of Burgundy,
And visited so frequently
At his court that soon the duchess
Began overtly to profess   48
Affection for him, so much so
That he would never have been slow
At understanding what she meant,
Had he not been all intent   52
On his own lady. In vain the duchess
Smiled at him; he did not guess,
For all her courtesy and guile,
He'd won her love. After a while   56
She was vexed enough to cast
Prudence aside, and at last

Came to him with this straightforward
Speech: "It seems to me, my lord,   60
As indeed to all your friends, your true
Merit should encourage you,
Brave and courteous as you are,
To seek a love that may seem far   64
Above your station; you would do well
To try." "My lady, what you counsel
Never would have crossed my mind!"
She said, "In fact I am inclined   68
To caution you against delay,
If some great lady should betray
An interest that you inspire
Beyond what friendship would require."   72
He said, "You must forgive me, lady,
But I really fail to see
What you mean to say and why.
Neither count nor duke am I,   76
And I have never looked above
My place for some exalted love,
Nor has anyone expressed
The slightest hint that such a quest   80
Would be rewarded with success!"
"Greater marvels have nonetheless
Been true, and may well be again.
Suppose I were to ask you, then: 84
Are you really unaware
That I myself might come to care
Enough, perhaps, to offer you
My love?" He said, "I never knew   88
Of this, my lady, but I would
Rejoice indeed if your love could
Be mine in honor. Only I pray
That God will keep me far away   92

From any love that might neglect
My obligation to respect
My noble lord; it would be vile
Treachery should I defile   96
His honor by a sinful deed."
She angrily replied, "Indeed!
I never would have taken you
For such fool. Who asked you to?"   100
"Of course you had no such intent,
My lady; that's just what I meant!"

Then the duchess said no more,
But bitter rage and hatred for   104
The chevalier was like a challenge
In her heart to seek revenge.
And so when she lay beside
Her husband that same night, she sighed   108
And after a while began to weep
Before the duke could go to sleep.
Soon, of course, he wanted to know
What it was that grieved her so,   112
And insisted she reply.
She said, "I have good cause to cry,
When I see how hard it is
For any man to winnow his   116
Enemies from loyal friends.
Honored above innocence,
Treachery goes without rebuke."
"In God's name, lady," said the duke,   120
"I can't imagine why you say
So strange a thing, but this you may
Well believe: I'll entertain
No traitor, if I know his name!"   124

"Then, my lord, you must refuse
To welcome X . . . , who has abused
Your honor and my own all day,
In the hope I would betray   128
Your love and favor his instead.
He never dared to speak, he said,
But kept his love in silence long.
It seemed to me I would do wrong   132
Not to speak of this to you.
It might very well be true
That he spoke no idle word
To me today—we've never heard   136
That anyone has caught his eye;
Perhaps this is the reason why.
I hope, for your honor's sake,
That you will not be slow to take   140
Measures against his insolence."
Said the duke, "For this offense
He'll answer to me, be sure of that!"

The duke felt such displeasure at   144
Her words that all night long he lay
Awake. He loved the chevalier,
But now believed his wife, and grieved
To think that he had been deceived   148
By one he trusted. So he spent
A sleepless night and next day sent
Immediately for the one
The duchess had accused of treason,   152
Although she was herself to blame.
Alone with the chevalier, he came
Directly to the point, and said:
"Just how far I was misled   156

By looks and valor I can see
Now, for without loyalty,
You have ill deserved your place
Of honor here, and your disgrace   160
Comes in answer to my love.
I believed you far above
Any such hypocrisy.
Even now I cannot see   164
How it happened that you cared
So little for my trust you dared
Make your treacherous appeal
To my own wife, and try to steal   168
Her honor and her love. To find
Betrayal of a baser kind
One would look far. You are forever
Banished from my lands! If ever   172
Anyone sees you here again,
You will be captured by my men
And take your rightful place among
Traitors—I will have you hung!"   176
When the chevalier had learned
Of what he was accused, he burned
With rage and trembled, well aware
Of what he'd lose by leaving there—   180
How could he see his love in case
He was exiled? In this place
Only could he safely stay
Close to her and make his way   184
In secret to his happiness.
He was, apart from this, no less
Dismayed because his noble lord,
Whom he in all good faith had honored,   188
Called him a traitor and a thief.

He felt his life was over, his grief
Was so intense. "By God above,
My lord, I could not be guilty of   192
What you suppose. Not in any way
At any time could what you say
Be true; it is only vile
Slander!" "There is no denial   196
Possible, and no defense.
Don't speak to me of innocence
When she has herself revealed
How you hoped that she would yield   200
To your desire, and how you went
And pleaded with her to consent;
Perhaps she kept back what you could add."
"My lady said what she is glad   204
To have you believe." "And I advise
You not to waste my time with lies!"
"There is no way for me to speak
In my defense; and yet to seek   208
A proof of what I did not do,
That nothing you heard was ever true,
I swear I'd give my very life!"
The duke remembered what his wife   212
Had said, her final argument
That made the truth seem evident:
The knight had not been known to care
For any woman anywhere.   216
He said, "If you insist, despite
All I know, that you are right,
You will give your solemn word
That what I ask you will be answered   220
Honestly; I can be then,
According to your reply, quite certain

Whether or not what I suspect
Is true. You cannot protect   224
Yourself in any other way."

By this time the chevalier
Was ready to promise anything,
If only he could somehow bring   228
The duke at last to realize
That he had been misled by lies.
Wishing at all costs to remain
Near the chatelaine's domain,   232
He most willingly agrees
To whatever it may please
The duke to ask. In his distress
He doesn't even try to guess   236
What the duke might want to know;
Feeling no guilt, he is not slow
To pledge his word. The duke, convinced
Of his sincerity, begins: 240
"You know that I would be inclined
To doubt a story of this kind;
Until now I've never yet
Had any reason to regret   244
My loving confidence in you.
I would not have listened to
The duchess with such great concern,
Were there not evidence to turn   248
Suspicion to your falsity.
I can't imagine you to be
Indifferent to love, indeed
Your face, your elegance, would lead   252
Whoever saw you to assume
There was somewhere a lady whom
You loved; yet we have never heard

Of any woman you preferred.   256
This is enough to make me feel
Sure that my wife did reveal
The truth to me: you have betrayed
All honor, hoping to persuade   260
The duchess to reward your shame
With secret love. If you still claim
This false, I ask you now to swear
You love someone, and tell me where   264
And who she is. Otherwise,
You're proved a traitor; I advise
You never to set foot here again!"

The chevalier only then   268
Realized he could not prevail.
Any argument would fail
In this debate. If he were to tell*
The truth, he might just as well   272
Be exiled, for he had no doubt
That if his lady should find out
He had broken faith with her,
She would be lost to him forever.   276
But in case he should decide,
Honoring his vow, to hide
His love, the duke would then believe
Him guilty; and, forced to leave,   280
Exiled on pain of death from love,
He'd suffer what he fears above
All else. He can't forget he owes
To this one lady all he knows   284
Of happiness. Should her embrace
Be forfeited by his disgrace,
Or because he was too weak
To keep his promise, he would seek   288

In vain a reason to forgive
That failure, or go on and live
Without her. In misfortune he
Was like the chatelain of Couci,   292
Who, with love and sorrow strong
Within his heart, composed this song:

Now Love grown cruel takes away from me
The sweet attentions of that dearest one   296
Who was my joy and who was perfectly
My lover and in all things my companion.
Remembering the pleasures I have known,
Her words of love, her simple courtesy,   300
There is no end to grieving but to die,
My heart and body severed willingly.*

The chevalier in his despair
Cannot decide if he would fare   304
Better if he were to tell
The truth or let the duke expel
Him from the land and yield to lies.
The tears of anguish in his eyes,   308
While he wonders how to speak
In his defense, run down his cheek.
But this infuriates the duke,
Who finds another way to rebuke   312
The knight: he does not wish to share
The secret of a love affair.
Abruptly he says, "Your sorrow,
Chevalier, only serves to show   316
What confidence you have in me.
You believe, apparently,
That I am apt to give away
Your secret. I can only say   320

I'd let my teeth be one by one
Pulled out before I'd ever have done
So vile a thing." "My lord, I swear
By God above, I do not dare   324
Answer you, whatever must
Become of me. I cannot trust
Anyone; I'd rather die
Than lose what I will lose if I   328
Should tell the truth. For if it were
Ever to be known to her
That I so basely was untrue . . . "
The duke replied, "I swear to you   332
On my very life and soul, I know
How to keep the faith I owe
To one who pledged me fealty.
What you have to say to me   336
Will never be by fault of mine
Revealed, nor shall any sign
Of what I know escape me while
I live." The chevalier on trial   340
Was weeping. "I will tell you then.
I love your niece, the chatelaine
Of Vergi, and she loves me in return."
"Do you claim that I'm the first to learn   344
Of this? Someone must have suspected.
If you want your secret protected,
Tell the truth! Someone must have known!"
"No one but ourselves alone,   348
Till now." "But it's beyond belief!
Without help you would come to grief,
And quickly, if you left to chance
The time and place of your romance."   352
"My lord, I've nothing more to hide
From you," the chevalier replied.

And so he told him how and when
He went to see the chatelaine,   356
And all about the promise made
To her, and how the small dog played
His part. "I won't be satisfied
Just by hearing how you hide   360
Your love. I insist that when
You go to see my niece again,
You take me with you. That way I
Once and for all can verify   364
Your story; and there is no need
For my niece to know." The knight agreed,
Saying, "If you are so inclined,
The truth is that I have in mind   368
To visit the chatelaine tonight."
The duke said that would be all right
With him; the journey, he was sure,
Would bring him both relief and pleasure.   372

In the place they had selected
They met at nightfall undetected.
The lady lived not far away;
On foot they quickly made their way   376
Into the orchard near her manor.
They scarcely had arrived before
The little dog was seen to race
Through the shadows toward the place   380
Where they were standing, and the knight
Welcomed him with great delight.
Then the duke, as they had agreed,
Lets the chevalier proceed   384
Toward his lady, quietly goes
After him, and pausing close
To the window of her bedroom, hides

As best he can. A tree provides   388
The shelter of great branches bent
Down as if it were a tent
Within which he could safely stay.
From there he saw the chevalier   392
Entering the room, and then,
Through a courtyard, the chatelaine
Coming toward him. The duke was near
Enough so that he could hear   396
Her joyful welcome as she ran
To meet her lover and began
Embracing him, her arms around
His neck. They had scarcely found   400
Breath to speak a word before
They'd kissed a hundred times or more.
The knight embraced her once again
And said, "My lady, my sweet friend,   404
My love, my dearest hope, my heart,
There is no happiness apart
From you in all the world for me;
And I have hungered so to be   408
With you like this, it seems a year
Since the last time I was here."
And she to him: "My lord, my dearest
Friend, my only love, the rest   412
Of time, each hour of every day
Is emptiness with you away;
But now that I can see you here
Beside me, there's no more to fear   416
From sorrow—you are safe and sound
And welcome indeed!" "And you well-found!"
Close to the door, the duke heard
All they said, and every word   420
Gave him reason to rejoice.

He recognized his niece's voice
And her face; he knew beyond all doubt
His wife had lied to him about   424
The chevalier. The evidence
Proved his good faith and innocence,
For if he loved the chatelaine,
He was unlikely to have been   428
Urging the duchess to betray
Her lord. The duke prepared to stay
Keeping watch, all through the night,
While the lady and the knight   432
In her chamber, wide awake
In bed, were well content to make
The most of time and celebrate
Their love. Nor shall I relate   436
More about their happiness;
Words alone are powerless
To tell the pleasures Love may give
To perfect lovers, those who live   440
Obedient to her commands.
What the true lover understands
Remains a mystery for those
To whom Love does not disclose   444
Herself, and never otherwise
Can they be made to realize
That love's unshadowed joy is worth
More than anything else on earth.   448
But those who for one moment wake
To love will never again mistake
The false for true; if love should last
Forever, yet when it is past   452
It will have been too brief. One night
Could last a week, the week might
Become a month, the month might be

A year, and if the year were three,   456
And three years twenty, which became
A hundred, it would be the same
For true lovers, who would pray
Still that the morning might delay   460
The chevalier had thoughts like these,
Remembering his joy would cease
All too soon, his night must end
Before the dawn. The chatelaine   464
Came with her lover to the door
To say farewell, and so once more
The duke could see them give and take
Kisses of love. Their voices break   468
Now with heavy sighs, and tears
Are falling as the moment nears
When the chevalier must go.
He turns away, and she with sorrow   472
Left alone begins to close
The door, but while she can she follows
With her eyes the one whom she
Would rather herself accompany.   476

The duke left his hiding place
As soon as the door was closed, to retrace
His steps, following the knight,
Who was lamenting that the light,   480
Approaching now, caused him to be
Expelled from happiness. While she,
Having been left behind, complained
Like him that night had not remained   484
A shelter for their love, deceiving
Joy; and the lady, grieving,
Had no praises for the day.
The knight continued on his way   488

With these same sad thoughts and words in mind.
But the duke, who was not far behind,
Caught up with him and joyfully
Embraced him, saying, "I will be   492
Your friend now and forevermore
In faithful love! All that you swore
Has been proved—and I could not afford
To be uncertain." "Thank you, my lord,   496
For that! But in God's name I pray
That you will never give away
The secret of what you have learned
Tonight. My joy would all be turned   500
To bitter grief if ever it
Were known, and with my love I'd forfeit
Life itself." The duke replied,
"You need not ask again. I'll hide   504
Your secret; no one will have heard
Of this from me. You have my word."

Talking together, they returned
To the castle. No one at all had learned   508
Of their adventure, but it seemed
At dinner that the duke esteemed
The chevalier now even more
Than he had ever done before.   512
The duchess, at this, was so offended
That, hiding her anger, she pretended
Illness, and quickly left the table.
She went to bed, but was unable   516
To find there any rest or pleasure.
Meanwhile her husband dined at leisure,
Washed his hands, and then remained
To see his guests were entertained.   520
After a time he visited

His wife, had her sit up in bed,
And asked that no attendant stay
With them in the room. When they   524
Were left alone, the duke inquired
Why the duchess had retired
In such a hurry during dinner
And what it was that troubled her.   528
She said to him, "By God, I swear
I was completely unaware
Until I sat down to that meal
That you could ever so reveal   532
Yourself unwise. You're not concerned,
Apparently, by what you learned
From me—you seem to take delight
In honoring the very knight   536
Who courted me behind your back!
And when you showed me such a lack
Of courtesy I had to leave,
To hide my anger here and grieve."   540
"Ha!" the duke replied, "My dear,
Not one word more do I wish to hear
Against that knight, either from you
Or anyone else. It is not true   544
That he ever had the least intent
Of courting you. He is innocent.
I know beyond the slightest doubt
He never even thought about   548
Such treachery—but on that score,
I don't intend to tell you more."

With these words the duke withdrew,
Leaving her deep in thought. She knew   552
That his refusal to explain
Meant that forever she'd remain

In torment, trying to understand
What had happened. On the other hand,   556
She thought that there must be a way
To make her husband give away
His secret. And the duchess waited
Impatiently and calculated   560
How she could best deploy her charms
When she would have him in her arms
That night; he would not be slow
To tell her what she wanted to know   564
If she could question him in bed.
And when the duke retired, instead
Of greeting him, she looked annoyed
And turned away as to avoid   568
His lying close to her. She knew
That if she wanted to subdue
Her husband, she need but display
Resentment, and in such a way   572
As to discomfit his desire.
He kissed her, only to inspire
Bitter reproaches as she cried,
"I will not be satisfied   576
With empty gestures, when I know
Too well what lies behind your show
Of love, how much you have deceived
My faith in you. Oh! I believed   580
For long, with foolish innocence,
That there was more than vain pretense
In your fair words when you so often
Said you loved me. But I've been   584
Disabused this day forever;
Now I can be sure you never
Loved me in your heart." "But why
Do you say that?" And she, to try   588

To win him over to her will,
Answered, "You told me to be still,
When I would have questioned you
About something it wouldn't do,   592
It seems, to have me know." "But tell me
What you mean!" "Whatever he
Found to make you take for fact
The lies behind which he attacked   596
My honor! But I don't want to hear
His story now; it's all too clear
How much you value loyalty
And love. In my sincerity   600
I've told you right away whatever
I learned, regardless if it were
Good or bad. But now I feel
Poorly repaid, for you conceal   604
Your thoughts from me. And rest assured
That I, from this day on, am cured
Of trusting you, and never more
Can I love you, as before,   608
With all my heart." And then she wept
As sadly as she could, and kept
Sighing as if her heart would break,
So that the duke began to take   612
Pity on her. "My dearest love,"
He said, "nothing stands above
Your happiness, nor would I give
You cause for anger. But forgive   616
Me this one time. I must refuse
To tell you what you ask, or lose
All honor." Quickly she replied,
"My lord, you are quite right to hide   620
Your secret from me; I'll betray
Your trust—that seems to be the way

You think of me! But truly I'm
Astonished; you can't name a time   624
When I was tempted to disclose
Anything you ever chose
To tell me, and no matter how
Small or great it was. Now   628
In all good faith I say to you
That while I live, I'll never do
So vile a thing." And once again
She wept. The duke, who had by then   632
Become uneasy and distressed,
Held out no longer. He caressed
Her lovingly and said, "My lady,
I really don't know what should be   636
My answer, but I do believe
That you would loyally receive
My confidence, and that no secret
Should come between us two. And yet   640
Remember this: should you betray
A word of this affair, you'll pay,
I swear it, with your life!" "My lord,"
She answered, "I can well afford   644
The risk; what could persuade me to
Break a promise I'd made to you?"
And the duke, because he held her dear,
Believed that his wife must be sincere,   648
And told her everything he'd learned
About his niece: how she returned
The knight's true love, and how he went
Himself and witnessed her consent.   652
In detail the duke related
Everything: how they had waited
In the orchard, what it meant
When the little dog was sent,   656

And how the chevalier had gone
To meet his love and stayed till dawn.
When the duchess realized
Her proffered love had been despised   660
For one whose rank was well below
Her own, she felt a mortal blow
Had been inflicted on her pride.
But she was careful still to hide   664
Her feelings from the duke, and promise
Never to breathe a word of this
To anyone, at any time,
"Or else," she said, "for such a crime   668
I should be hung!" Even then,
Hatred for the chatelaine
Filled her heart; she had begun
Already to plot against the one   672
Because of whom the knight abused
Her pride and, to her shame, refused
Her love. Now the duchess thought
Only of revenge, and sought   676
How best to profit from the hour
When it would be in her power
To whisper in the lady's ear
Something she would grieve to hear.   680
But the duchess was denied
Her vengeance until Whitsuntide,
A feast the duke would celebrate
By holding his full court in state.   684
Messengers telling what he planned
Went out to the ladies of the land,
And the first of his requests
Was that his niece be among his guests.   688
The duchess's blood ran cold when she
At last approached her enemy,

In her eyes the most hateful thing
In all the world; and yet dissembling   692
What she felt, she greeted her
More graciously than she had ever
Done before. And to express
The rage within her heart, the duchess   696
Waited until Whitsunday.

That evening, when they took away
The tables to prepare the hall
For dancing, she invited all   700
The ladies to her room, where they
Could in privacy array
Themselves in honor of the dance.
The duchess, when she saw her chance,   704
Delayed no longer but addressed
The chatelaine, as if in jest:
"Be sure to look your best, my dear,
Since your handsome friend is here!"   708
Untroubled was her prompt reply:
"My lady, I can't imagine why
You would hint at such a thing.
I'd have no friend who would not bring   712
Honor to my lord; never yet
Have I been willing to forget
My own." She said, "I have no doubt
Of that. I wonder, though, about   716
Your special talent in the art
Of training dogs to act a part!"
The other ladies overheard
But couldn't understand a word.   720
With the duchess they departed
For the dance, which had just started.

The chatelaine remained there
Alone and sick from her despair 724
And raging anger. Churning inside,
She found a room where she could hide;
No one would be there. But instead,
A little maid lay close to the bed. 728
The lady did not see her. She thought
She was alone, and so, distraught
By bitter grief, let herself fall
Upon the bed and mourned for all 732
Her happiness. "O God, have mercy!
What am I to do? If she
Taunts me so that I regret
Training my little dog, the secret 736
Never could have been revealed,
Except by him who made me yield
To love and now casts me away.
For that he never would betray, 740
Unless he was so much her friend
He wished our love were at an end,
To put her in my place. The fact
Is all too clear—he broke the pact 744
We made, and how can I suppose
He loves me still? And yet, God knows,
I loved him more than anything
On earth, and love can never bring 748
More joy. Nothing had the power
To drive him from my thoughts each hour
Of every day and every night;
He was my pleasure, my delight, 752
My comfort and my happiness.
Absent, he was nonetheless
Close to me, within my heart!

Ah, dearest friend, would you depart?   756
How can it be that you have changed
So much that you yourself arranged
For love to end in treachery?
I thought you were more true to me   760
Than ever Tristan to his fair
Iseut, and in return I swear
That twice as dear to me you were
As I was to myself. And never   764
At any time, from the first day
We loved, did I in any way
Give you the least cause to so
Hate me that you'd lightly throw   768
Our love away as you have done,
Telling our secret to someone
Whom you prefer to me. Alas,
My love, how could this come to pass,   772
When I have always been so far
From being disloyal, as you are;
If God above had offered me
The world, the very sky to be   776
My own, and with it Paradise,
I would not take it if the price
Were losing you, my only treasure,
My very health and all the pleasure   780
Of my life. Nothing grieved
Or troubled me while I believed
You had the slightest love for me.
Alas for love! To think that he   784
Would make me come to this despair!
When he was with me, all my care
Was for his pleasure; I required
Only to do what he desired   788

To be content. And he would say
That nothing could banish him away
From me, that body and soul he was
My love, my own forever. Because   792
His words were gentle, I believed
All he said, so well deceived
I thought his heart could not be closed
In hatred toward me—not to boast   796
The love of a duchess or a queen.
How good it was when I could lean
Against him, with my heart on his,
When I could believe his promise   800
To be, while he remained alive,
My love—and I would not survive
His death, were it to come before
My own; it would have been a more   804
Cruel fate to be condemned
To see him no longer than to end
My life with his. Alas for love!
By what right did he tell her of   808
Our happiness? Why did he choose
Deliberately so to lose
My love? He knew that he had vowed
To me before I first allowed   812
His visits that they would be concealed
From everyone, and should he yield
The secret, it would mean the end
Of love between us. It has happened   816
So. And yet how can I live,
Mourning for him? Life can give
Nothing now but further pain;
I have no reason to remain   820
Alive without him. Rather I pray

To God for death, and that He may
Have mercy on my soul and bless
My lover, by whose pitiless   824
Cruelty I have been driven
Now to death. I have forgiven
His treachery. Nor do I grieve
That I must die, for I receive   828
My fate from him; remembering
The sweetness of his love, the sting
Is drawn away from death." The lady
Said nothing after that, but only   832
Sighed and, just before the end,
Murmured, "God keep you, dearest friend."
And with these final words she pressed
Her arms hard against her breast,   836
Fainting in agony. All trace
Of color vanished from her face;
Her heart was still, and she lay dead.

Her lover did not know. Instead   840
He had been dancing at the ball,
Waiting for her. But nothing at all
Could please him when he was denied
The presence of his love. He tried   844
To find out why she didn't appear,
Whispering in the duke's ear,
"My lord, why does your niece delay
So long to come and dance today?   848
It must be something she has done
That made you lock her up in prison!"
The duke, who had not been aware
That the chatelaine was not yet there,   852
Looked for her among the dancers
All in vain. And so he answers

The knight by leading him away
Toward his niece's room. When they   856
Cannot find her, he suggests
They try the dressing room, and requests
The chevalier to look for her
Alone, knowing he would prefer   860
To find his lady in a place
Where privately they might embrace.
Gratefully the knight accepts
The opportunity, and steps   864
Into the alcove where she lies
So pale and still. With joy he tries
To waken her to his caress;
Her lips are cold, and colorless   868
Her face, her body rigid. So,
In agony, he came to know
The truth. "O God! Why did she die?
What could have happened?" At his cry,   872
The maid who was hidden near the bed
Suddenly appeared and said,
"My lord, this much I know is true.
She prayed for death because she knew   876
That she was by her love betrayed,
From some remark the duchess made,
Teasing her about her friend
And how she trained a dog. In the end   880
The lady's bitter grieving broke
Her heart." The knight, as she spoke,
Realized that he had killed
The chatelaine himself, and filled   884
With wild remorse, he cried his pain
Aloud: "Oh my sweet love, in vain
Were you so loyal, you above
All on earth deserving love,   888

And by this vile betrayal brought
To death. Justice would have sought
To be avenged on me alone,
But you would in my place atone   892
My falsity. Now let me pay
For treason in the only way
I can." With that he took a sword
Down from the wall and drove it toward   896
His heart. The chevalier had fallen
Over her lifeless body when
His blood ran out and he was dead.

The little serving maid, who fled   900
In terror when she saw the two
Had died, told everything she knew
As soon as she found the duke. She kept
Nothing back: how she had slept   904
Inside the alcove and remained,
While the chatelaine complained
Of her lost love, and how the duchess
Caused the lady such distress   908
By mocking her, and how she died
Of her despair. Horrified,
The duke hastened to behold
The truth of what he had been told.   912
From the knight's breast he withdrew
The sword, then in the hall broke through
The dancers circling there to find
His wife. Not in the least inclined,   916
Now, to engage in lengthy speech,
He wanted, in his rage, to teach
The duchess he meant what he had said;
He raised his sword and struck her head   920

Without a single word. At his feet
The duchess fell. And then complete
Confusion filled the hall. No one
Could understand what the duke had done,   924
What they all had seen with their own eyes—
For the joyful dancers a sad surprise.
Then, to the people of his court,
The duke gave a full report,   928
Telling of the promise made
And broken and again betrayed.
Tears came to their eyes, and when
They saw the lovers, they wept again,   932
And there was the duchess lying dead.
Saddened, angry, they soon fled
The court and all the horror they
Were witness to. The duke, next day,   936
Had the lovers placed within
A single grave, and buried in
Another place his wife. Alone
With sorrow, he was never known   940
To laugh again. He took the cross,
Became a Knight Templar across
The sea, and never more returned.
Ah, God! If all their love was turned   944
To bitterness and grief, the reason
Lies in what the knight had done,
Believing that he should entrust
The duke with what he knew he must   948
Conceal from all, or sacrifice
His love. Nothing could suffice
Ever to free him from the promise
He had made. Surely this   952
May be a warning to all those

Who love, never to disclose
Their secret, for by that they gain
Nothing, and while they remain   956
Undiscovered, those who prey
On others' love are kept at bay.

Notes to the Poems

PHILOMENA

9   The narrator here responds to an unidentified interlocutor who appears from time to time in the text, usually to ask a question or to make a comment. In lines 401–51 and 481–96 he engages the narrator in a discussion of the nature of love, which then merges into the continuing story.

29–30   Where Ovid named the Eumenides, Chrétien evokes one of them, Tesiphone (Chrétien de Troyes, *Philomena: Conte raconté d'après Ovide,* ed. C. de Boer [Geneva: Slatkine Reprints, 1974], 98), along with Atropos, the Fate who cuts the thread of life.

40   Tervagant is named in *La Chanson de Roland* as one of the pagan deities.

134   Charles Homer Haskins indicates that Cato's *Distichs* were often included in twelfth-century introductory readers; they were much prized moral verses. *The Renaissance of the Twelfth Century* (Cleveland: Meridian Books, 1963), 131–32.

169   Alice M. Colby's summary of the ideal portrait corresponds in almost every detail to the description of Philomena; it features "long, gleaming blond hair divided by a straight parting; a reasonably large, smooth white forehead; finely drawn dark eyebrows with a wide space between them; sparkling eyes; a bright face; a rosy, youthful complexion; a straight, well-formed nose that is not very large; a small mouth with moderately full red lips and small white teeth not separated by wide spaces; a long neck; gently curving shoulders; long straight arms; white hands with long slender fingers; a white bosom with little breasts; a small waist; and slender sides and hips." *The Portrait in Twelfth-Century French Literature* (Geneva: Droz, 1965), 69.

176   Apollonius of Tyre is the protagonist of a Latin romance that was very popular in the Middle Ages. Apollonius won the friendship of a king by his skill at playing ball; he later gave music lessons to a princess (as Tristan would). The mention of this book seems particularly appropriate in the context of *Philomena,* since both are concerned with rape.

Tristan's enthusiasm for chess caused him to be captured by pirates. His knowledge of games in general is mentioned in Jean Renart's *Reflection,* lines 104–5.

178–79   These seem to have been dice games, which were, as Colby writes, "important in courtly society as a source of entertainment at social gatherings" (*Portrait,* 132).

184   Colby cites authorities to explain the distinction, which would have been obvious to a medieval listener, between more easily trained hawks, like the falcon, and those, like the lanner, which may refuse to attack game. Daniel J. Brimm, raptor conservationist, tells me that the lanner will fly right up to its quarry and then turn aside (hence the word "balk" in my translation). These details of Philomena's skill at falconry are particularly interesting because there is, to my knowledge, no other literary portrait of a medieval lady that credits her with more than the ability simply to carry a hawk on her fist.

186   Hawks molt yearly and require greater care when they cannot fly. The skilled falconer can speed the process so that the bird is sooner ready to hunt again.

189–93   Because the fabrics named (*diaspre* and *baudequin*) are elaborately patterned and the verb *ouvrer* is somewhat vague—it can mean any kind of needlework, including both weaving and embroidery (Colby, *Portrait,* 135)—it is difficult to understand what skills are being praised. The costly fabrics would most likely have been imported, but Colby may be right in understanding Chrétien to be making the extraordinary claim that Philomena could produce them herself.

The *mesniee Hellequin* would have been particularly difficult to portray, whether in or on the cloth, since it probably represented "a band of souls in purgatory who, when driven about in the night, were visible because of the fiery envelope or phosphorescent glow surrounding their bodies" (ibid., 136). Nancy A. Jones adds that the image "alludes to the transformed states of Tereus, Progné, and Philomena. Their bird forms locked in eternal flight

and pursuit suggest sin's abasing effect and its infernal or purgatorial punishment" ("The Daughter's Text and the Thread of Lineage in the Old
French *Philomena*," unpublished article, 28). "Hellequin" ultimately lost its
ghostly quality and became "Harlequin."

200   A *vielle* is a stringed instrument played with a bow, a prototype of
the violin.

233   Chrétien's "pagan law" permitting incest is, needless to say, a pure
invention. It would seem intended to diminish the enormity of Tereus's behavior; since a sister-in-law is almost a sister, his desire was almost licit. See
Introduction, 10 above.

278   E. Jane Burns points out the importance of this question to which
the story provides an unexpected answer (*Bodytalk* [Philadelphia: University of Pennsylvania Press, 1993], 117–18).

402   *Amor* is a feminine noun.

458   This is one of the passages that seem to blame Philomela for
Tereus's passion.

590   Dining tables on trestles were brought into the hall when required and covered with cloths.

736   Despite the best efforts of medievalists, most of whom now attribute *Philomena* to Chrétien de Troyes, there has not been a satisfying explanation of the name given here: Crestiiens li Gois (line 734 in Boer's edition). Boer proposed that Gois, possibly modern Gouaix, could have been
Chrétien's native town. *Gois* is most probably pronounced *gwaice;* hence the
English rhyme *place/Gois.*

812–39   The rhetorical flourishes are reminiscent of Chrétien's more
mature eloquence, as in Yvain's declarations of love for Laudine.

1051   Here Chrétien conflates the Christian and pagan views of hell.

1070   Ovid suggests that Tereus may have raped Philomela again after
tearing out her tongue, but he does not visit her after that. Chrétien writes,
literally: "her life was a burden to her, and every day her sorrow was renewed
by the traitor, the vile demon who was inflamed by love of her, and it *dis-
pleased* her greatly that the one who had betrayed her *was taking* his pleasure of
her by force" (italics mine). The italicized verbs, *despleisoit* and *feisoit,* are in the
imperfect tense, which suggests continued, rather than concluded, action.

1101   In the *Metamorphoses* both Arachne and Philomela were weavers,
and Chrétien uses the verb *tisser,* to weave, in this passage (line 1117 in the

Old French), although no loom is mentioned. Old French lines 1094–95, however, say that the equipment available would permit Philomena to make a *cortine* (bed curtain) *ouvree,* which I have translated as "embroidered fabrics." Chrétien's vague indications would be consistent with that, although others have understood that Philomena was weaving a tapestry. In a private communication, Nancy A. Jones noted that twelfth-century weaving techniques would not have been adequate to make elaborate narrative designs, whereas embroidery techniques were far more advanced; the eleventh-century Bayeux "tapestry" is in fact an embroidery. Chrétien's use of *tisser* may be more a reference to the classical tradition than a precise definition of Philomena's work. But cf. note to lines 189–93.

1133   The word translated here by "raped" is *esforça.* The verb *esforcer,* Kathryn Gravdal points out, was used in the twelfth century to mean both "to strive admirably" and, when used with an object, "to rape" (*Ravishing Maidens* [Philadelphia: University of Pennsylvania Press, 1991], 3). By the seventeenth century, only the former meaning remained, and *viol* was used to signify rape.

I have also translated *maumetre* (Old French line 1164) and *afoler* (line 1327) as "rape" and "defile" (lines 1170 and 1323). This sense is clearly justified by the context, but the definitions of these verbs are much less specific. Only the larger dictionaries include *violer* among their synonyms.

1134   The verb used is *escrire,* to write. Similarly, in Marie de France's *Nightingale,* line 136, the message is "A or brusdé e tut escrit" (embroidered in gold and completely written over).

1449   The description of the modern *huppe fasciée,* found in France, coincides remarkably with Ovid's description of the "Epops" (hoopoe): it has upright feathers on its head and a very long, curved beak. A large bird, it is often found on the ground, and its aspect is both comical and warlike. In Chrétien's description the hoopoe loses any dignity it might have had, becoming small and ugly.

I am grateful to Nancy Vine Durling for sending me a picture of the *huppe fasciée* from a French bird book.

1467   The cry of the nightingale as it is expressed in Old French is *oci,* "kill" (see Introduction, 12). Thus the songbird comes to resemble one of Philomena's hawks.

THE NIGHTINGALE

49–51   Some have interpreted this passage to mean that the lady was watched when her husband was at home, but it seems more logical to assume that *cil* refers to the lover when *he* was at home, that is, not at tournaments.

138   The cloth was *tut escrit,* which could mean either that it was covered with the gold embroidery or that the message was written or depicted on it. In any case, there was an oral message as well, conveyed by the messenger.

THE TWO LOVERS

26   Robert Hanning and Joan Ferrante's translation in *The Lais of Marie de France* (New York: E. P. Dutton, 1978) gives a note to this passage with additional lines from other manuscripts, which add that the princess had rich suitors, but her father loved her too much to agree to a marriage. Her excessively loving father calls to mind Philomena's.

97   Salerno was one of the earliest medical centers in Europe, and its women practitioners were often mentioned.

HONEYSUCKLE

40   Whitsuntide is Pentecost, the traditional time for King Arthur to hold his court and for chivalric adventures to begin.

53   See the Introduction, 16, on the ambiguity of Tristan's inscription.

61–62   I take these lines ("Ceo fu la somme de l'escrit / Qu'il li aveit mandé e dit") to refer to an earlier message. Others believe they refer to the message on the *bastun,* or stick, which she would understand either from the name alone or in code.

107–11   These lines have been accurately translated if they suggest the determined ambiguity of the original.

113   In the Tristan episode of a thirteenth-century continuation of Chrétien's *Perceval,* Tristan, in disguise, identifies himself to Iseut by playing the

Lai du Chievrefueil on a small flute. She is at first angry, thinking that Tristan had taught someone else "the *lai* that he and I composed." Then she realizes that the musician is Tristan himself. Gerbert de Montreuil, *La Continuation de "Perceval,"* ed. Mary Williams, vol. 1 (Paris: Champion, 1922), lines 4066–4088.

LANVAL

12   On Whitsuntide, see note to line 40 of *Honeysuckle,* above.

38   This sentence has often been taken as an indication that Marie was living in England when she wrote *Lanval.*

63   Jean-Claude Aubailly says that the gold basins are a specific attribute of the *fées,* and by their content, water, symbolize purification and rebirth (*La Fée et le chevalier* [Paris: Honoré Champion, 1986], 87). Marie says nothing further about them, although she promises to do so. Perhaps the "truth" about the basins is the truth about the *fée,* which is the story itself.

87   The cost of things, the social importance of money, is a major theme in *Lanval.* Lack of money was an issue for Lanval at the beginning of the story, but money no longer matters to him once he has it.

254   The polite way of "holding hands" was to place the open fingers against those of one's companion, as in the dance scene reproduced as the frontispiece of this book.

456   That is, first Lanval must swear that he did not try to seduce the queen, and then he can offer proof that his statement about his love's beauty was factual and not malicious.

507   This remark could mean either that the arrival of the ladies distracted them or that they wondered whether it should have an effect on the case.

562   In his edition Alfred Ewert mentions, but does not adopt, the reading *chainse* instead of *chainsil* in manuscripts C and P (Marie de France, *Lais* [Oxford: Basil Blackwell, 1952], 175). Eunice Rathbone Goddard, however, notes that in Karl Warnke's editions of 1900 and 1925 *chainsil,* which she defines as a fine linen, "has been changed to the preferable reading *chainse*" (*Women's Costume in French Texts of the Eleventh and Twelfth*

Centuries [Baltimore: Johns Hopkins University Press, 1927], 77). My translation, "shift," is based on that reading.

602   *Gariz* can mean anything from "cured" in the physical sense to "saved" in the religious or judicial sense. I understand Lanval to be saying that he asks for nothing beyond the grace of her presence, and does not hope for forgiveness.

603   The *fée* is usually referred to as *pucele,* a maiden. But when her messengers arrive at Arthur's court, they refer to her as *dame,* a lady (493). To rescue Lanval, the *fée* must condescend to participate in a realm where worldly values dominate. Marking that transition, the narrator here says, "La damë entra al palais" (Ewert, line 601). When she leaves the palace, *la dame* is again *la pucele* (630).

ELIDUC

16   The text says she was the daughter of the king and queen, but the latter is not mentioned again. In *Philomena* and *The Two Lovers,* the mother is also not part of the story, except by implication.

125   The constable was the chief military officer of the king's household.

1050   The use of personal pronouns in this passage is indicated, although not imposed, by the identification of the first weasel as the *cumpagne* of the other. Hanning and Ferrante, in their translation of the *Lais,* suggest that although the weasel who finds the flower is male and "seems to represent Eliduc, the 'flower' *he* finds to bring her back to life is his wife's charity" (225n. 9).

THE REFLECTION

22   In Jean Renart's *L'Escoufle* (The Kite), the destruction of this bird both avenges the unhappiness caused by Guillaume's earlier encounter with it and allows his return to good fortune.

39   The Old French refers to L'Eslit, usually identified as Miles de Nanteuil, bishop of Beauvais, to whom Jean Renart dedicated *Guillaume de Dole.*

48a   In his edition of *Le Lai de l'ombre* (Edinburgh: Edinburgh University Press, 1948), John Orr adds this line, which appears in other manuscripts of the poem, in order to suggest the meaning of an otherwise obscure passage; hence the triple rhyme. See also Margaret Winters's edition (Birmingham, Alabama: Summa Publications, Inc., 1986), 79.

90–91   The text says literally that the knight wished that there were two Mondays in every week (that being the usual day for a tournament to begin).

96   *Vair* was fur from the belly of the squirrel, often used with the darker fur from the back. In the earliest versions of the tale, Cinderella's slipper must have been made of *vair*, which in time came to be understood as *verre* (glass).

125   Tristan once succeeded in visiting Iseut by disguising himself as a madman. The story is told in the *Folie Tristan*.

146–51   Scholars have been uncertain about the meaning of this passage, but the general idea is that the knight, having fallen in love with the lady at first sight, now evokes the memory of her beauty to justify his emotions.

161   Winters, in her edition of the poem, notes that this is the oldest French reference to barbers as surgeon-dentists (82–83).

270   "To the ladies, knights!" This variation on the traditional war cry "To arms!" also occurs in *Guillaume de Dole*.

386   The Old French reads, literally, "by drawing a feather across my eyes." A similar expression is used in *Guillaume de Dole*.

422–37   In a variant to this passage, women are reproached for being flirtatious; Sarah Kay concurs with this opinion ("Two Readings of the *Lai de l'Ombre*," *Modern Language Review* 85 [1980]: 523). I find the passage reminiscent of one in Chrétien de Troyes's *Yvain*, in which knights are considered to lack sophistication when they mistake warm greetings from ladies for an expression of love (ed. Wendelin Foerster [Manchester: Manchester University Press, 1952], lines 2459–63).

457   Tristan, near death from a wound, has himself placed in a rudderless boat; the sea takes him to Ireland, where he is cured by Iseut and her mother.

527   "Pleasure" translates *preu*, which here means something like "profit" or "advantage." The knight's service to her, his displays of valor in her honor, would give her no pleasure, since she does not love him.

669   Cîteaux was the founding house of the austere Cistercian order.

686–87   The Old French reads literally, "So I won't go and take him by his beautiful hair."

700–705   The apparent incoherence of the text at this point may be intended to express the lady's state of mind.

716   Literally, "she didn't receive a fist blow close to her ear." *Guillaume de Dole* contains a similar expression.

815   "Renart" refers to Renard the Fox, whose eloquence won him many a prize. Jean Renart alludes to him several times in *Guillaume de Dole,* and in ways that suggest a reference to himself as well. Renart might, of course, have been his pseudonym.

836–37   The proverb translated says that one shouldn't press so hard on a crust of bread that the soft part underneath jumps out.

858   This line, considered by both Orr (59) and Winters (94) to be merely padding, seems to me a complement to lines 62–63, in which the author claims not to know the knight's name. Here Jean Renart uses a pretext to point out that the lady is not to be named either.

912   The Old French says that she is *toz reverdis,* all green again (like the trees in springtime).

962   The mysterious final line reads, "Contez, vos qui savez de nombre." Lewis Thomas elucidates the connection between relating stories and numbers: "An account is in one sense a tale, a narrative; so is the recounting of a story. Both derive from *count,* which is in its first sense a numbering of items in a set, a reckoning. To count is also an affirmation: I count myself lucky. . . . Latin produced *computare,* to calculate, compute together, and this became Old French *cunter, conter,* and Old English *count,* a reckoning. The words *account* and *recount,* with their meaning of narrating tales, seem to have carried this sense simultaneously." *Et Cetera, Et Cetera: Notes of a Word-Watcher* (New York: Penguin Books, 1990), 41–42; I am grateful to Helen Ranney, M.D., for making me aware of Thomas's work on etymology.

THE CHATELAINE
OF VERGI

38   The idea that the room might not be empty is the only suggestion that she might have a husband, except for the chatelaine's reply to the

duchess in line 713. The lord she refers to there could possibly be the duke but is more probably her husband.

271   This passage expresses the alternative possibilities as a *geu parti,* a debate conducted in verse. I do not know that Leigh Arrathoon is correct in stating that "the entire poem is structured around" this literary form, but he is right to point out the presence of the technical term (Old French line 269), which seems to undercut the knight's anguish at his dilemma. *The Lady of Vergi,* ed. and trans. Leigh A. Arrathoon (Merrick, New York: Cross-Cultural Communications, 1984), xx.

302   By virtue of this stanza's appearance in the *lai,* the châtelain de Couci, a twelfth-century poet, became a fictional hero, and in the eighteenth century acquired as his partner the châtelaine de Vergi herself. The practice of quoting a poem in this manner was initiated by Jean Renart in *Guillaume de Dole.*

Designer: Janet Wood
Compositor: G & S Typesetters, Inc.
Text: 11 point Garamond
Display: Dorchester, Garamond
Printer/Binder: Thomson-Shore, Inc.